**FRIENDS
OF ACPL**

JUN 1 4 2007

The Case of the Green River Killer

by Diane Yancey

LUCENT BOOKS

An imprint of Thomson Gale, a part of The Thomson Corporation

THOMSON
™
GALE

Detroit • New York • San Francisco • New Haven, Conn. • Waterville, Maine • London

For more information, contact
Lucent Books
27500 Drake Rd.
Farmington Hills, MI 48331-3535
Or you can visit our Internet site at http://www.gale.com

LIBRARY OF CONGRESS CATALOGING-IN-PUBLICATION DATA

Yancey, Diane.
  The case of the Green River Killer / by Diane Yancey.
    p. cm. — (Crime scene investigations)
  Includes bibliographical references and index.
  ISBN-13: 978-1-59018-955-9 (hard cover : alk. paper)
  1. Serial murders—Washington (State)—Green River Region (King County)—Case studies—Juvenile literature. 2. Ridgway, Gary Leon, 1949-—Juvenile literature. 3. Serial murder investigation—Washington (State)—Juvenile literature. 4. Serial murderers—Washington (State)—Green River Region (King County)—Psychology—Juvenile literature.
  I. Title. II. Series: Crime scene investigations series.
  HV6533.W2Y36 2007
  364.152'30979777—dc22

                                                                    2006007164

ISBN-10: 1-59018-955-8
Printed in the United States of America

Contents

Foreword

The popularity of crime scene and investigative crime shows on television has come as a surprise to many who work in the field. The main surprise is the concept that crime scene analysts are the true crime solvers, when in truth, it takes dozens of people, doing many different jobs, to solve a crime. Often, the crime scene analyst's contribution is a small one. One Minnesota forensic scientist says that the public "has gotten the wrong idea. Because I work in a lab similar to the ones on *CSI*, people seem to think I'm solving crimes left and right—just me and my microscope. They don't believe me when I tell them that it's the investigators that are solving crimes, not me."

Crime scene analysts do have an important role to play, however. Science has rapidly added a whole new dimension to gathering and assessing evidence. Modern crime labs can match a hair of a murder suspect to one found on a murder victim, for example, or recover a latent fingerprint from a threatening letter, or use a powerful microscope to match tool marks made during the wiring of an explosive device to a tool in a suspect's possession.

Probably the most exciting of the forensic scientist's tools is DNA analysis. DNA can be found in just one drop of blood, a dribble of saliva on a toothbrush, or even the residue from a fingerprint. Some DNA analysis techniques enable scientists to tell with certainty, for example, whether a drop of blood on a suspect's shirt is that of a murder victim.

While these exciting techniques are now an essential part of many investigations, they cannot solve crimes alone. "DNA doesn't come with a name and address on it," says the Minnesota forensic scientist. "It's great if you have someone in custody to match the sample to, but otherwise, it doesn't help. That's the investigator's job. We can have all the great DNA evidence in the world, and without a suspect, it will just sit on the shelf. We've all seen cases with very little forensic evidence get solved by the resourcefulness of a detective."

While forensic specialists get the most media attention today, the work of detectives still forms the core of most criminal investigations. Their job, in many ways, has changed little over the years. Most cases are still solved through the persistence and determination of a criminal detective whose work may be anything but glamorous. Many cases require routine, even mind-numbing tasks. After the July 2005 bombings in London, for example, police officers sat in front of video players watching thousands of hours of closed-circuit television tape from security cameras throughout the city, and as a result were able to get the first images of the bombers.

The Lucent Books Crime Scene Investigations series explores the variety of ways crimes are solved. Titles cover particular crimes such as murder, specific cases such as the killing of three civil rights workers in Mississippi, or the role specialists such as medical examiners play in solving crimes. Each title in the series demonstrates the ways a crime may be solved, from the various applications of forensic science and technology to the reasoning of investigators. Sidebars examine both the limits and possibilities of the new technologies and present crime statistics, career information, and step-by-step explanations of scientific and legal processes.

The Crime Scene Investigations series strives to be both informative and realistic about how members of law enforcement—criminal investigators, forensic scientists, and others—solve crimes, for it is essential that student researchers understand that crime solving is rarely quick or easy. Many factors—from a detective's dogged pursuit of one tenuous lead to a suspect's careless mistakes to sheer luck to complex calculations computed in the lab—are all part of crime solving today.

A Twenty-Year Quest

The case of the Green River killer opened when two boys on bicycles spied a fully clothed body floating in the placid waters of the Green River near the city of Kent, Washington, on July 15, 1982. The police were called in, examined the scene, and identified the victim as Wendy Coffield, a runaway teenager. They found nothing to indicate who had strangled her before dumping her body in the water. She had last been seen on July 8, 1982.

Less than one month later, on August 12, 1982, the body of another young woman was found slumped over a log in the Green River in the same vicinity. Police were again called in and identified the remains as those of Debra Bonner, a young prostitute who worked in the region. She, too, had been strangled before being left in the water. She had last been seen on July 25, and the King County medical examiner estimated she had been dead for three weeks.

Just three days after the discovery of Bonner, a river-rafter named Robert Ainsworth came upon the bodies of two more women floating just under the surface of the Green River in about the same spot. Ainsworth notified the police, who sealed off the area, began searching for evidence, and quickly found another body lying in the grass on the riverbank less than 30 feet (9m) away. The women in the water were identified as Marcia Chapman and Cynthia Hinds; the one on the bank was sixteen-year-old Opal Mills. Chapman had been dead one to two weeks, Hinds three or four days, and Mills just thirty-six hours. Detective David Reichert, who assisted in all the recoveries, remembers, "I was already wondering about the person . . . who was responsible for this little horror show. We all were trying

The discovery of four bodies on the banks of the Green River near the city of Kent, Washington, marked the beginning of a twenty-year search for a killer.

Sixteen-year-old Opal Mills was one of the earliest victims of the Green River Killer.

to imagine how someone would have handled the chore of lugging the bodies to the water. . . . And naturally, we speculated about the connection to the girl . . . Debra Bonner, who had been pulled from the river within sight of this spot."[1]

Because the killings had many aspects in common—the victims were all young women from the fringes of society who had been strangled and dumped in the river—King County police established a task force to investigate them on August 16. The members followed leads, sifted through evidence, interviewed suspects, and gathered a massive amount of information in the course of their investigation. Despite their efforts, however, the killer or killers always managed to elude them.

The killing continued, too. By the end of 1983 at least thirty women were missing or dead, and bodies were regularly being found. The media had become critical and the victims' families were impatient for an arrest. Reichert defended the task force's efforts: "Nothing is harder than finding a bad guy who attacks strangers and knows how to hide his tracks. I know this isn't much [comfort] to those who have lost loved ones. But it's a fact that when we're dealing with the most skilled type of killer, we often need more time, and more luck, than anyone can imagine."[2]

Cold Case

Despite all the hard work, no quick arrest was made in the case. The killings appeared to stop by the late 1980s, however. Many people became convinced that the killer was either dead, behind bars, or had moved to another part of the country. Similar strangulation murders of young women in places such as Portland, Oregon, and San Diego, California, supported the latter theory.

Although the case went cold—unsolved and on the books—for ten years it was not forgotten by the victims' families or the task force. The latter had been reduced to just one

What's in a Name?

Dispute has arisen over who coined the term "serial killer." Both FBI agent Robert Ressler and former King County detective Robert D. Keppel claim to have used it first in the 1970s. Both men agree on a definition, however. Serial killers are individuals who commit at least three murders during distinct episodes with periods in between when they appear normal—go to work, interact with their families, and so forth. They frequently have a sexual motivation for carrying out the killings.

The term *serial killer* separates murderers who claim multiple victims over a long period of time from those who kill multiple victims all at once. The latter are known as mass murderers. Dylan Klebold and Eric Harris, who shot and killed twelve students and a teacher at Columbine High School in Colorado on April 20, 1999, are examples of mass murderers. Like Klebold and Harris, mass murderers are often motivated by depression, anger, and/or mental illness and sometimes commit suicide after their attacks.

Spree killers are similar to serial killers in that they commit multiple murders in different locations over a period of time. Unlike serial killers, however, spree killers do not have "normal" periods. Andrew Cunanan was a spree killer who murdered five people, including designer Gianni Versace, during a three-month period in 1997. Cunanan left a trail of bodies from Minneapolis to Florida and committed suicide before authorities could capture him.

member in 1991, but that one investigator, Detective Thomas Jensen, continued to push ahead, correlating evidence and managing tips. He also kept track of developments in genetic technology, hopeful that it might someday be used to help catch the killer. Such proved to be the case. In 2001 science advanced to a level that allowed genetic material left on some of the Green River victims to be linked to a suspect, an individual so mundane and mild-mannered that his confession shocked the country. "In most cases, when I murdered these women, I

Man with a Secret

For almost twenty years, King County police tried to solve the Green River case. As authors Carlton Smith and Tomas Guillen write in their book The Search for the Green River Killer, *the difficulties were intensified by the colorlessness of the person they hunted.*

At the beginning, there was only the man. He drove alone, keeping his thoughts to himself. It was as if he existed outside of the rest of the world, isolated inside his own skin, captivated by his own thoughts. He was a man with a face so common, so ordinary, that no one thought to look to see what was within. He passed by others quietly, as if he were not even there, and no one saw him at all. But he was a man with a secret, and the secret was death.

His favorite time was the afternoon. In his truck, the man drove on the highway, looking, choosing, selecting. He made it a rule to drive until he found what he wanted, waiting for him by the side of the road. When it was right he would stop, and the game would begin.

Carlton Smith and Tomas Guillen, *The Search for the Green River Killer.* New York: Signet, 2004, p. 1.

did not know their names," he stated. "Most of the time, I killed them the first time I met them and I do not have a good memory for their faces. I killed so many women I have a hard time keeping them straight."[3]

The killer's confession, coupled with his decades-long killing spree, makes the Green River story more compelling than many fictional tales. The vulnerable victims, untiring investigators, and incalculable suspects all played their parts in a case that was the longest unsolved serial murder investigation in U.S. history. Even the ending was surprising and left many shaking their heads. King County prosecutor Norman Maleng, who had made the victims and their families his priority, summed up most people's feelings in the following words:

> When I see the face of justice in this case, it is those young women that I see. They deserve to have the truth of their fates known to the world. When I see the face of justice in this case, I will see each family impacted by these crimes. They deserve to know the truth about the fate of their loved ones. . . . Finally, the face of justice reflects our whole community. We have all suffered this terrible trauma known as the Green River murders. We deserve to know the truth and to move on.[4]

CHAPTER 1

The Victims: Daughters of the Night

The five women discovered near the Green River in 1982 alerted police to the fact that a serial killer was on the loose in their region. The knowledge gave some a feeling of having been through such a nightmare before. In 1974 serial killer Theodore "Ted" Bundy had lived in the vicinity, too, stalking and murdering young women for several months before moving on to Utah and Florida. Bundy, however, had focused on college coeds who had standing in the community and were not prone to disappear without warning. The majority of the Green River victims were prostitutes, individuals who were particularly vulnerable to anyone who wanted to prey upon them. Authors Carlton Smith and Tomas Guillen write, "On the run from abusive or otherwise dysfunctional homes, alienated from familiar friends and places, confused about life, frightened of authority . . . , these juveniles were perfect victims."[5]

The Strip

At least four of the first five victims of the Green River Killer had worked as prostitutes along "the Strip." The Strip was a section of Highway 99, also known as Pacific Highway, that ran north and south between the cities of Seattle and Tacoma, Washington. The highway was a local thoroughfare that people used as they went to and from work every day. It was lined with restaurants, gas stations, car dealerships, mini-marts, and small strip malls. The Strip, which ran through the little city of Des Moines and past the Seattle-Tacoma (SeaTac) International Airport, was one of the highway's seediest sections, characterized by taverns, twenty-four-hour cafés, and cheap motels.

The Strip was well known in 1982 for its thriving sex trade. Even in the early afternoon, young women in short skirts, tight jeans, and high-heeled boots could be seen standing on the roadside or in parking lots, waiting to catch the eye of passing drivers. Smith and Guillen write, "Literally hundreds of women shouted, waved, gestured, and pantomimed their wares on the stretch of highway that ran from the beginning of The Strip at South 139th Street and extended south to about South 272nd Street, a distance of perhaps ten miles."[6]

Most prostitutes on the Strip preferred "car dating,"—having sex in the car— because it saved time and allowed them to get back on the street more quickly. Thus, when a customer, known as a "john" or a "trick," pulled over, she would climb

Nighttime on "the Strip," one of Pacific Highway's seediest sections, could be dark and threatening for young prostitutes in the 1980s.

By the Numbers

35

Number of serial killers estimated to be active in the United States at any particular time

into his vehicle and the two would drive to an out-of-the-way spot. There were many such spots just off the Strip. The airport had expanded its runways beginning in 1975, so authorities had purchased thousands of houses in nearby neighborhoods over which the noisy jets would be landing and taking off. The owners had moved away, the houses had been boarded up or removed, and the yards had become overgrown. These abandoned neighborhoods with their silent, dead-end streets proved perfect places for the women to spend a few moments with their clients.

Prostitutes who worked the Strip migrated to and from other disreputable areas in western Washington, too. First Avenue in Seattle was known as "Flesh Avenue," because of the many women who worked it, while a six-block stretch of Pacific Avenue in Tacoma to the south housed dozens of clubs and taverns that were a haven for prostitutes, gamblers, and drug dealers. The police in these cities lacked manpower to shut down the illegal activities, and those women who were arrested usually paid a fine and were back on the streets in a day. Reichert notes, "The community didn't press us to make cleaning up The Strip [and other areas] a priority. . . . A great many viewed prostitution as a victimless crime."[7]

On the Streets

Even if they had had the manpower, police had few legal means of getting the youngest prostitutes, many of whom were teenage runaways, permanently off the street. The Washington State Juvenile Justice Act of 1977 had given minors new rights. In particular, it legalized the act of running away. Police officers who located a runaway at the parents' request often found that the teen refused to return home. Because officers had many

other crimes to deal with, they usually took a runaway report from parents and simply filed it. Only if a parent was insistent was the report followed up with a search. As a result, in the 1980s an estimated six hundred teens, male and female, lived on the streets of Seattle and King County alone.

Many were there because their home life was unhappy or unsettled. Delise Plager, for instance, had grown up in group homes and other facilities after being taken away from her alcoholic mother. Keli McGinness had been abused and raped before she ran away and turned to prostitution.

Other teens were on the street as a result of their own unwise decisions. Tracy Winston came from a loving home, but she fell in love with an ex-convict when she was sixteen and became a prostitute to support him. April Buttram became rebellious when she entered her teens. She used drugs and alcohol and focused on parties rather than school. Her parents loved her but could not tolerate her behavior. "One night," her

In the 1980s an estimated 600 teens, male and female, lived on the streets of Seattle and King County, Washington, alone.

15

mother remembers, "I caught her crawling out of the window, carrying a suitcase. . . . I just told her, 'At least have the guts to go out the front door.' And she did. And she never came back."[8]

A Vulnerable Lifestyle

Once involved in the prostitution lifestyle, most of the women drifted from place to place, addicted to drugs and alcohol, trying to make a quick dollar as they struggled to survive. They stayed in cheap motels, often with a boyfriend that kept an eye on them when they were on the street. Many became pregnant and ended up with a child to support.

All were open to attack, simply because they went to remote spots with men who were willing to take advantage of them. Some of these men were mentally ill or had their inhibitions lowered by drugs or alcohol. All were willing to break the law. It was common for a woman to be raped and beaten, and often she was the victim of theft.

Despite the danger, all avoided the police as much as possible to escape arrest. They hid their real identities by taking street names and changing them often. For instance, Debra Estes was known on the streets as "Betty Jones." Kimberly Nelson went by Tina Tomson, Kris Nelson, Linda Lee Barkey, and sometimes simply "Star." After being arrested a number of times, they moved to other cities, such as Los Angeles or San Francisco, where they were unknown to the police. Usually they left without a word to anyone. One girl, who prefers to remain nameless, points out, "When a girl was gone for a while, I didn't pay attention—because I figured they'd gone to Seattle or Alaska. Funny how we assumed they just went on with their lives."[9]

The Killing Continues

Seventeen-year-old Gisele Lovvorn was lucky enough to have a boyfriend that reported her missing just one day after she met the killer on the Strip. Raised in an upper-middle-class family in California's San Fernando Valley, Lovvorn, who was very intelligent but unhappy with herself and her life, had run away from home when she was fourteen. The next three years she hitchhiked around the country, calling her parents from places like Fargo, North Dakota, and Cut Bank, Montana. Eventually she linked up with an older man who promised to protect her but in fact encouraged her to work as a prostitute to support their hand-to-mouth lifestyle.

On July 17, 1982, they were living in a tiny apartment off the Strip when Lovvorn went out in the afternoon to engage in prostitution. The deaths of four other prostitutes had been in all the papers, but Lovvorn paid no attention to that. Being from out of town, she perhaps did not connect the fact that she was in the vicinity where the victims had last been seen. When she did not return to her apartment that evening or the next day, her boyfriend called the police, but little effort was made to find her. She appeared to have vanished into thin air.

Family members like Michelle Blair, sister of victim Gisele Lovvorn, lived for years without knowing if the Green River Killer would ever be caught.

Then, on September 25, a man riding a dirt bike through the deserted neighborhoods south of SeaTac airport smelled a foul odor. Following his nose, he peered under some bushes and saw a decayed, nude body with blond hair. A call to the police brought out a team of investigators. It was Lovvorn, and she had been strangled with a pair of men's socks that were still around her neck. Although she had not been dumped in the river, her age, occupation, the area she worked, and the manner of her death put her in the same category as the earlier victims. The newly formed Green River Task Force informed the press that Lovvorn had become the sixth victim of the mysterious murderer's campaign.

Area of disappearances

The King County Sheriff's Office yesterday announced the arrest of a suspect in connection with the killings of these four women, who are among the 49 victims police attribute to the Green River killer. The majority of victims disappeared from this stretch of Highway 99 near Seattle-Tacoma International Airport. The colored squares show where most of the victims were last seen.

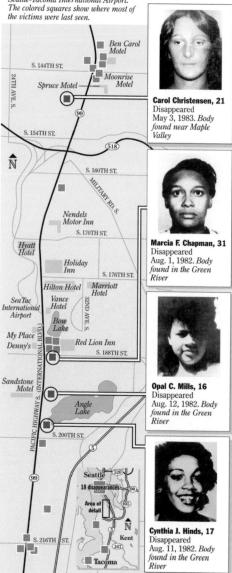

Carol Christensen, 21
Disappeared
May 3, 1983. *Body found near Maple Valley*

Marcia F. Chapman, 31
Disappeared
Aug. 1, 1982. *Body found in the Green River*

Opal C. Mills, 16
Disappeared
Aug. 12, 1982. *Body found in the Green River*

Cynthia J. Hinds, 17
Disappeared
Aug. 11, 1982. *Body found in the Green River*

MICHELE LEE McMULLEN / THE SEATTLE TIMES

An article in The Seattle Times *gives readers information about where many Green River victims were last seen.*

Missing, Believed Dead

Several months passed before another body was found, leading police to wonder if the killings had stopped. In fact, although few were aware of it, other prostitutes had vanished and continued to vanish regularly throughout 1982. Terry Milligan disappeared on August 29, Mary Meehan disappeared on September 15, Debra Estes on September 20, Denise Bush on October 8, and Shawnda Summers on October 9.

Every month in 1983 another girl was reported missing. Three went missing in April alone. Sandra Gabbert, who worked the Strip and Kimi-Kai Pitsor, who had just begun working the streets in downtown Seattle, disappeared within hours of each other on April 17. No one knew for certain that they had fallen prey to the killer because their bodies could not be found. Nevertheless, the task force and the missing girls' families viewed the situation with sinking hearts.

Then Carol Christensen was found strangled on May 3. Police did not know if they were looking at the killer's work or not. Christensen was discovered by a family hunting for mushrooms in the woods 20 miles (32km) east of the Strip. Like the earlier victims, Christensen had been young and had worked at the Barn Door Tavern on the

Strip. Unlike any of the others, however, her body had been fully dressed and posed after death. After some debate, her name was added to the Green River Killer victims' list. Analysis of genetic material found on her body eventually proved that the decision to include her was correct.

Dump Sites

After the discovery of Christensen, the remains of women who had been reported missing in 1982 and 1983 began to be found regularly, indicating that the murderer had gone through a veritable killing frenzy during those years. Most of the remains were only bones, found clustered in isolated sites where the killer had felt safe depositing one victim after another. Eight such sites were eventually identified.

An investigator looks for remains of a victim of the Green River Killer.

One lay in a deserted neighborhood north of the SeaTac airport. There the remains of two women were found in August 1983 and another in March 1984. A second cluster lay south of the airport near where Lovvorn's body had been found. Investigators discovered the remains of three women there in October and November 1983. A fourth was found there in October 1989.

In September 1983 the chance discovery of human bones by a man looking for a lost chicken near Star Lake, west of the towns of Kent and Auburn, revealed another cluster. The remains were those of Gail Mathews, a prostitute who had disappeared from Pacific Highway in April 1983. A few months later a mushroom hunter stumbled over a skull in the same area. It was identified as the skull of Terry Milligan, who had disappeared in 1982. A search of

Vanished!

The young prostitutes who vanished from the Strip in the 1980s were unique individuals with hopes, dreams, and stories to tell. Crime writer Ann Rule describes one of them, Constance Elizabeth Naon, in her book Green River, Running Red.

Constance Elizabeth Naon, twenty, drove a fifteen-year-old Chevrolet Camaro that she often parked at the Red Lion [Hotel] at 188th [St.] when she was working the street. She was a lovely young woman with perfectly symmetrical features, and she did pretty well financially, but she had a drug problem that ate away at her money. She also had a straight job at a sausage factory, and on June 8, [1983,] she planned to pick up her paycheck there. She called her boyfriend to say she was on her way to visit him and would be there in twenty minutes. She never arrived.

Police found her Camaro in the Red Lion lot late in June. It was dusty and cluttered with Connie's possessions, but there was nothing in it that could tell them where she was or what might have happened to her.

Ann Rule, *Green River, Running Red*. New York: Free Press, 2004, p. 112.

the Star Lake area revealed three more sets of remains. A fourth was discovered in the same region a year later.

Two more clusters were found in heavily overgrown areas of forest off Interstate 90, a freeway that wound through the Cascade Mountains east of Seattle. One site discovered in early 1984 by a timber company employee yielded the remains of three women. Another site just down the highway held the bones of three more.

Remains were found hidden as far away as Oregon. In June 1985 a backhoe operator was preparing land to become a tree farm near Tigard, Oregon, south of Portland. He turned up human bones that were eventually linked to Denise Bush and Shirley Sherrill, who had disappeared from Seattle in 1982. Later in 1985 the remains of two more women were found in Tualatin, south of Portland.

The Killer's Choice

As the bodies were discovered and identified, the investigators noticed that the killer did not seem to care about race when he chose his victims. The women were Caucasian, black, Asian, and Native American. In other ways they were similar, however. Most were very young—more than half were under the age of twenty-one. Three had been only fifteen when they died. This meant that they had not been out on the street for very long and were inexperienced in fending off danger. Reichert notes, "Young and hardened, they mistakenly believed their 'street sense' would protect them."[10]

Many were small in stature. Mills's nickname had been "Peanut," because she was so petite. Debbie Abernathy, whose body was found east of Enumclaw in 1984, was just 5 feet (1.5m) tall and weighed 90 pounds (41kg).

Most had been pretty. Carrie Rois, who disappeared between March and June 1983, could have passed for a cheerleader. McGinness, who went missing in June 1983, was a striking blond who had been in high demand on the Strip. According to one friend, she "was at the top of the ladder of the girls on the street."[11]

The Witness

When trying to trace the last movements of the victims, there was usually little information for the task force to go on. A girl would be seen one moment and then, a few minutes later, have vanished into thin air. In early May 1983, however, a man named Robert Woods reported an incident that would later prove significant.

Woods reported to the Des Moines Police Department that he saw his girlfriend, Marie Malvar, get into a truck with a man on the night of April 30. The truck was a dark color with a primer spot where repairs had been made. Woods did not tell the police that Marie was a prostitute. He merely explained that when the driver of the truck pulled out onto the street, Woods followed in his car. He lost sight of the truck when it made a left turn against a light, but as the light changed, Woods turned left and tried to catch up with it. The pickup had disappeared. Woods had not seen Marie since that night.

The police took Woods's report, but made no promises. Thus, a few days later Woods and Marie's father and brother decided to go looking for the pickup, starting at the place it had disappeared. They reasoned that, because it had seemed to vanish off the highway so quickly, the driver might live in a nearby neighborhood.

Their search took hours, but finally, in a secluded cul-de-sac, they saw a maroon truck with a primer spot. It was parked in the driveway of a home similar to all the others in the area—modest and middle-class. Because the house lay in the city of Des Moines, the men again called the local police, who went out to interview the owner. He insisted that he knew nothing about a missing woman. Taking his word, the police told Woods and the Malvars that they must have been mistaken. The three men had to be content with that. Woods had no proof that the Green River Killer had taken Marie, but he never saw her again, and her name was eventually listed as one of the Green River victims.

Close Call

Malvar had not been able to escape her fate, but nineteen-year-old Rebecca Guay was more fortunate. She came forward in 1984 and told the task force that she had been assaulted two years previously while she was working as a prostitute on the Strip. Although she had no proof, she believed her assailant might have been the Green River Killer.

In November 1982 Guay's customer drove her to a dark neighborhood just off the Strip. After they got out of the

THE VICTIMS

Gary Leon Ridgway admitted to taking the lives of 48 women, all but four of whom have been identified. Many of their bodies were found in South King County, where Ridgway grew up, lived and worked. Most died in the 1980s, but Ridgway admitted to killing one woman just five years ago. He also told investigators that his earliest victim may have been killed in the 1970s. Here are the brief details about the 44 victims whose remains have been identified.

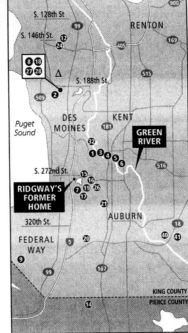

❶ Wendy Coffield
Age: 16
Missing: July 8, 1982
Found: July 15, 1982

❷ Gisele Lovvorn
Age: 17
Missing: July 17, 1982
Found: Sept. 25, 1982

❸ Debra Bonner
Age: 23
Missing: July 25, 1982
Found: Aug. 12, 1982

❹ Marcia Chapman
Age: 31
Missing: Aug. 1, 1982
Found: Aug. 15, 1982

❺ Cynthia Hinds
Age: 17
Missing: Aug. 11, 1982
Found: Aug. 15, 1982

❻ Opal Mills
Age: 16
Missing: Aug. 12, 1982
Found: Aug. 15, 1982

❼ Terry Milligan
Age: 16
Missing: Aug. 29, 1982
Found: April 1, 1984

❽ Mary Meehan
Age: 18
Missing: Sept. 15, 1982
Found: Nov. 13, 1983

❾ Debra Estes
Age: 15
Missing: Sept. 20, 1982
Found: May 30, 1988

❿ Linda Rule
Age: 16
Missing: Sept. 26, 1982
Found: Jan. 31, 1983

⓫ Denise Bush
Age: 22
Missing: Oct. 8, 1982
Skull found: June 12, 1985, in Tigard, Ore.
Body found: Feb. 10, 1990

⓬ Shawnda Summers
Age: 17
Missing: Oct. 9, 1982
Found: Aug. 11, 1983

⓭ Shirley Sherrill
Age: 18
Missing: Between Oct. 20 and Nov. 7, 1982
Found: June 14, 1985

⓮ Colleen Brockman
Age: 15
Missing: Dec. 24, 1982
Found: May 26, 1984

⓯ Alma Smith
Age: 18
Missing: March 3, 1983
Found: April 2, 1984

⓰ Delores Williams
Age: 17
Missing: March 8, 1983
Found: March 31, 1984

⓱ Gail Matthews
Age: 24
Missing: April 10, 1983
Found: Sept. 18, 1983

⓲ Andrea Childers
Age: 19
Missing: April 16, 1983
Found: Oct. 11, 1989

⓳ Sandra Gabbert
Age: 17
Missing: April 17, 1983
Found: April 1, 1984

⓴ Kimi-Kai Pitsor
Age: 16
Missing: April 17, 1983
Skull found: Dec. 15, 1983
Remains found: Jan. 1986

㉑ Marie Malvar
Age: 18
Missing: April 30, 1983
Found: Sept. 29, 2003

㉒ Carol Christensen
Age: 21
Missing: May 3, 1983
Found: May 8, 1983

㉓ Martina Authorlee
Age: 18
Missing: May 22, 1983
Found: Nov. 14, 1984

㉔ Cheryl Wims
Age: 18
Missing: May 23, 1983
Found: March 22, 1984

㉕ Yvonne Antosh
Age: 19
Missing: May 31, 1983
Found: Oct. 15, 1983

㉖ Carrie Rois
Age: 15
Missing: May 31 to June 13, 1983
Found: March 10, 1985

㉗ Constance Naon
Age: 21
Missing: June 8, 1983
Found: Oct. 27, 1983

㉘ Kelly Ware
Age: 22
Missing: July 19, 1983
Found: Oct. 29, 1983

㉙ Tina Thompson
Age: 22
Missing: July 25, 1983
Found: April 20, 1984

㉚ April Buttram
Age: 17
Missing: Aug. 18, 1983
Remains found: Aug. 30 and Sept. 2, 2003

㉛ Debbie Abernathy
Age: 26
Missing: Sept. 5, 1983
Found: March 31, 1984

㉜ Tracy Winston
Age: 19
Missing: Sept. 12, 1983
Found: March 27, 1986

㉝ Maureen Feeney
Age: 19
Missing: Sept. 28, 1983
Found: May 2, 1986

㉞ Mary Bello
Age: 25
Missing: Oct. 11, 1983
Found: Oct. 12, 1984

㉟ Pammy Avent
Age: 16
Missing: Oct. 26, 1983
Found: Aug. 16, 2003

㊱ Delise Plager
Age: 22
Missing: Oct. 30, 1983
Found: Feb. 14, 1984

㊲ Kimberly Nelson
a.k.a. Tina Tomson and Linda Lee Barkey
Age: 26
Missing: Nov. 1, 1983
Found: June 14, 1986

㊳ Lisa Yates
Age: 26
Missing: Dec. 23, 1983
Found: March 13, 1984

㊴ Mary West
Age: 16
Missing: Feb. 6, 1984
Found: Sept. 8, 1985

㊵ Cindy Smith
Age: 17
Missing: March 21, 1984
Found: June 27, 1987

㊶ Patricia Barczak
Age: 19
Missing: Oct. 1986
Found: 1993

㊷ Roberta Hayes
Age: 21
Missing: 1987
Found: Sept. 12, 1991

㊸ Marta Reeves
Age: 37
Missing: 1990
Found: Sept. 1990

㊹ Patricia Yellow Robe
Age: 38
Missing: 1998
Found: Aug. 6, 1998

SEATTLE POST-INTELLIGENCER
published November 6, 2003

Becoming a Homicide Detective

Job Description:
Homicide detectives respond to crime scenes for the purpose of solving murders. They obtain clues, gather evidence, investigate leads, question witnesses and suspects, conduct arrests, and testify at court trials. Their work hours are unpredictable and irregular. Officers are frequently expected to be armed and to exercise their authority whenever necessary, even outside working hours.

Education:
Potential homicide detectives are encouraged to obtain a bachelor's degree in criminal justice or law enforcement at a college or university. After graduation, new recruits attend police academies for twelve to fourteen weeks where they receive instruction in firearm use and safety, self-defense, first aid, civil and constitutional rights, and methods of investigation.

Qualifications:
Aspiring homicide detectives may begin their careers in a clerical or traffic patrol position. They are then promoted through the ranks as they gain experience and further training.

Additional Information:
Homicide detectives must have an interest in people and the ability to relate at all levels. They must be honest and responsible, able to withstand pressure, and able to make objective judgments in difficult circumstances. Good communication skills are important, as are good observational skills and the willingness to confront and resolve problems. Good physical health is a must.

Salary:
A homicide detective typically earns between $30,000 and $80,000 annually.

vehicle, he suddenly began strangling her. Guay managed to escape and ran to a nearby mobile home park for help. She did not call the police at the time, but she had seen her attacker's identification card and remembered where he worked. When the task force showed her a mug book of men who had been arrested for soliciting prostitutes, she identified a picture.

> **By the Numbers**
>
> # $10,000
>
> **1982–1983 budget for the Green River Task Force**

A member of the task force interviewed the man, who admitted that he had choked Guay, but only because she had bitten him and made him angry. The man was asked to take a polygraph test, but declined. Guay did not press charges, perhaps because she had been involved in an illegal activity or because she was afraid the man might take revenge on her. "This stuff . . . affected me so bad that it was hard for me to sleep at night," she says. "I had a fear of men for a long time. I was scared to death that someone was going to look for me and try to kill me."[12]

The man's name was placed in a police file and put aside. There were so many similar incidents being reported regularly that no one saw a reason to suspect that this was the man for whom they were all looking.

Loved and Mourned

Prostitutes like Guay were not the only ones who felt victimized by the Green River Killer. The families of the women lived with fear and anxiety, too. They knew that their loved ones were wrong to have gotten into such a dangerous lifestyle, but despite that, they knew that those loved ones had feelings, talents, strengths, and weaknesses that made each unique and precious. Gabbert's mother recalled that her daughter had been a star on the girls' basketball team before dropping out of high school. Meehan's family remembered her love of animals, and her boyfriend recalled that she had smuggled stray cats and dogs into their motel room on the Strip. As Reichert writes, "The women who were killed were not the caricatures . . . sometimes presented by the media. They were vibrant young people with hopes and dreams. They had been loved during the time they lived, and they were deeply mourned in their deaths."[13]

When a girl went missing, or when her remains were found, families anguished over the death. Some never recovered from their loss. For instance, Rebecca Marrero's mother had a nervous breakdown when years passed and neither her daughter nor her remains were found. Malvar's disappearance wrecked her parents' marriage.

Some families became bitter because the killer had not been caught and made to pay for his crimes. This fact also frustrated the investigators, many of whom ultimately devoted decades to the quest to catch him. From the beginning they had hoped to do so quickly. When that did not happen, they doggedly continued, intent upon beating the odds that predicted they would fail. Reichert writes, "There is no perfect crime and there are no perfect criminals. I was convinced that the Green River killer had eluded us mainly through luck, and I knew that kind of luck doesn't last forever. We were going to do our best to make sure it ran out soon."[14]

CHAPTER 2

The Investigation: Tracking an Elusive Killer

Reichert was a key player in the search for the Green River Killer. As a King County detective in 1982, he was on hand when the first body was discovered, and he helped bring the case to a close as the sheriff of King County over twenty years later.

Reichert was only one of many who hunted the killer over the years, however. The investigation involved a task force, made up of members of the King County Police Department (renamed the King County Sheriff's Department in 1998), Port of Seattle Police Department, Seattle Police Department, Pierce County Sheriff's Department, and Washington State Patrol. The King County Medical Examiner's Office played a large part in the case, as did the Washington State Patrol's crime laboratory. Also involved were members of the FBI, outside experts experienced in tracking serial killers, and a multitude of other people ranging from psychics to police in other states. Reichert writes, "We knew that it was important for us [the task force] to stay on good terms with other police departments, because the big breakthrough in our case was likely to be made by a street cop who had Green River in mind while he or she was performing routine duties."[15]

The Task Force

The original Green River Task Force was a twenty-five-member team of King County law enforcement personnel created in the summer of 1982 after the discovery of the first victims in the river. King County sheriff Bernard Winckoski and Major Richard Kraske, in charge of the King County Police

Department's Criminal Investigations Division, pulled the team into play as soon as they realized there was a serial killer at work in the area. Kraske handled planning and decision-making for the first two years of the investigation.

Each member of the team worked with wholehearted dedication. They put in double shifts. They followed up every tip. They interviewed families, friends, coworkers, and business owners on the Strip. They checked on men arrested for assaulting or threatening prostitutes. They talked with the victims' probation officers and with law officers in other cities.

Much information was gathered, but no clues pointed directly to one man. Some on the force even believed that they could be looking for more than one individual, either a team

Dave Reichert, pictured in 2004, was a key player in the search for the Green River Killer.

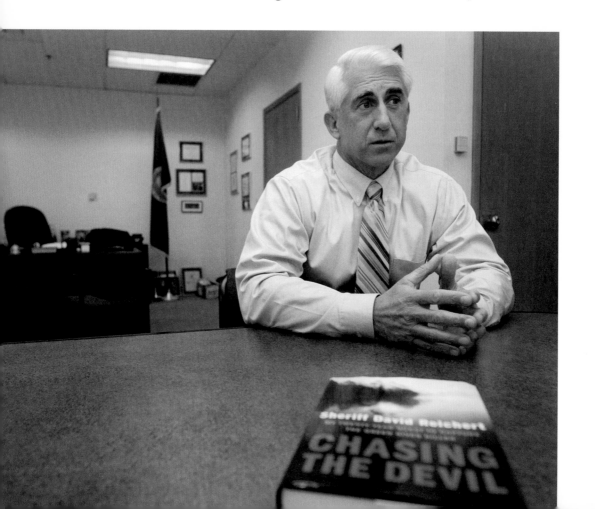

Processing a Murder Scene

1. **Interview:** One crime scene investigator must interview the first law enforcement officer at the scene and any witnesses to determine what allegedly happened, what crime took place, and how the crime was committed.

2. **Examine:** Investigators conduct an examination of the scene that includes identifying possible items of evidence, identifying the killer's point of entry and point of exit, and getting the general layout of the crime scene.

3. **Photograph:** The crime scene photographer takes pictures immediately and regularly throughout the investigation to retain a pictorial view of what the crime scene looks like and to record possible items of evidence.

4. **Sketch:** A member of the team completes a rough sketch to demonstrate the layout of the crime scene, to identify the exact position of the deceased victim, and to identify the exact position of possible evidence within the scene.

5. **Process:** The crime team identifies, evaluates, and collects physical evidence from the crime scene for further analysis in the crime laboratory.

of men or two separate murderers who were coincidently killing at the same time. To complicate matters, girls continued to go missing and bodies continued to be discovered, adding to the cases that needed to be worked. Frustrated, overworked, and under pressure to make an arrest, the investigators fought impatience and discouragement. Task Force member Bruce Kalin remembers, "It was depressing and stressful. All of us were tired all the time. We were sick all the time. It brought out the best and the worst."[16]

Bigger and Better

The case had not progressed far when Vernon Thomas was sworn in as sheriff of King County in April 1983. Thomas set out to get more money and support to enlarge the original task force. He also appointed veteran police officer Frank Adamson as the task force's commander. Adamson was a patient, persistent man who was known as a team builder. He was highly intelligent and inspired those under him with a sense that they could be successful. "I'm a facilitator. I'm a motivator,"[17] he explained when he took the job.

The enhanced task force began operations in January 1984, with the number of investigators expanded to thirty-six. Its office was relocated from downtown Seattle to the sheriff's spacious district office in Burien, south of the city, so investigators would be closer to the Strip.

Because the case was so complex, the team decided to use a three-part strategy that included investigating the victims and their backgrounds, keeping the Strip under surveillance, and investigating suspects. Adamson felt confident that the approach would soon uncover the murderer. "I honestly thought that because I had good people, we would have this thing solved within six months,"[18] he said.

By the Numbers

400,000

Pages of documents compiled during the Green River investigation (by 2001)

Crime Sites

Adamson was realistic enough to know that part of his team's time would be taken up processing recovery sites. That did not occur every day, but when a body was found, the locale had to be thoroughly searched. The killer seemed to prefer sites that were on steep hillsides in heavily forested areas. Washington's moist climate produced thick underbrush, and blackberry vines made some areas impassable. Despite the obstacles, the task force investigators became known nationwide as experts in how to meticulously work a crime scene.

First, they strung crime scene tape around the site to secure it from possible trespassers. Once they learned that the killer deposited his victims in clusters, they cordoned off a large area and brought in Explorer Scouts and other volunteers to

William Haglund was one of the medical examiners who was responsible for determining manner of death and identity of the victims in the Green River Killer case.

search for additional bodies. If more remains were found outside the cordoned-off area, the perimeter was extended to include them. Within the initial perimeter, a circle of tape marked each decomposition site—the place where each body lay. Another circle of tape was strung around the areas where each body might have been scattered by weather or animals.

Once the site was secure, access paths had to be cut through the brush and brambles so workers could come and go easily. These paths were marked with tape or planks. If the slope was steep, ladders were set up for investigators to use.

After that, each decomposition site was carefully inspected, sometimes over the course of three or four days. Photos and videos were taken at every step. Vegetation over and around the body was cut down and checked for evidence. Medical examiners Donald Reay and William Haglund, who were responsible for determining manner of death and identity of the victims, took careful notes as they examined the remains. They then supervised the collection and inventory of the bones. If any were missing, investigators searched for them on hands and knees. They also looked for trace evidence such as hair and fingernails with magnifying glasses and tweezers. They sifted the dirt under the remains through screens in order to retrieve the tiniest scraps. A metal detector was used in case they had overlooked any metallic objects, such as jewelry.

Evidence or Not?

While decomposition sites were being processed, other investigators searched the entire crime scene for evidence the killer might have left behind. This, too, was an extremely difficult task, because the killer chose sites where others had dumped trash and debris. Investigators had a hard time knowing whether articles such as rags and beer cans that littered the area were evidence or not. And when the skeleton of a large dog was found lying near one of the bodies at the Star Lake site in 1984, they were doubly perplexed. They wondered if the animal had come there by accident or if the murderer had killed

Some victims of the Green River serial killer were found near Star Lake.

it. They wondered whose dog it had been and if there was a message to be found in its presence there.

Once something was judged significant, it was photographed and then carefully placed in a bag to prevent contamination by other items. Each item was given a number and logged in order to correctly preserve it for a later trial. It was then transported to the crime lab for further analysis. Notes regarding when and where each was retrieved were reviewed and placed in the proper files.

Over the course of years, evidence found at each scene mounted up. By 1988 the task force had logged more than nine thousand items. Kalin says, "We had mountains of evidence. We even took birds' nests from scenes hoping we would find a hair from the suspect or a piece of jewelry."[19]

The Interviews

At the same time that part of the task force worked crime scenes, other members carried out other aspects of the investigation.

Ted Bundy on "The Riverman"

In 1984 Dave Reichert and Bob Keppel interviewed Ted Bundy to get insights into the mind and methodology of a serial killer. Bundy's assessment of the Green River Killer's demeanor, recorded in Keppel's book The Riverman, *proved surprisingly accurate when the killer was finally apprehended.*

My feeling about the guy is he's very low-key and inoffensive. My guess is he's got more than one approach to these girls. . . . If he were just some john driving in and snatching prostitutes, I think you would have caught him by now. But, like I say, I think he knows what these girls are like and what they need. . . . I've thought of the various ways he might approach them, even calling them on the phone. Let's say somehow he was able to contact them by phone—some of them, not all of them. I'm not saying he has one technique. In fact, he may not be a wizard, but he's bright enough to understand that he can't be approaching the same way every time. He knows that those areas [on the Strip] are under heavy surveillance, even under the best of times. But he was going back there after the heat was on. I was continually amazed by this guy's [guts]. I mean, after all the victims he snatched from Pacific Highway South, it seems that they continued to disappear from there. My guess is that he just blends into that environment—he may be a familiar-type character to that area. He may feel so comfortable with these type of women and understand them so well, he knows how to manipulate them.

Robert D. Keppel, *The Riverman.* New York: Pocket Books, 1995, pp. 232–33.

Some managed paperwork. Some followed up on tips regarding suspicious men or people who might know something. Thousands of such tips were phoned or mailed to the office in the course of a year.

Some members of the task force worked the Strip in an effort to spot the killer whom they believed could still be frequenting prostitutes there. They talked to business owners and customers at bars and taverns to see if they had seen or heard anything suspicious. They talked to every prostitute they could find, although they discovered that many remained fearful of talking freely to the police. Reichert writes, "Although a number of women were very cooperative and let us get close, others couldn't stop playing the same kind of games they used to fend off vice cops under more ordinary circumstances."[20]

Thousands of people on and off the streets were interviewed in the course of the investigation. Many were interviewed multiple times in the hope that they could provide additional information. Families were the most willing to help but often did not know or did not want to admit that their loved one had been a prostitute. Family interviews were difficult for the investigators because of the emotions involved. Not only were parents, brothers, and sisters worried, grief stricken, and angry, but they often focused that anger on the investigators who seemed to be getting nowhere.

The Specialist

Despite their hard work and dedication, leaders of the task force realized early in the investigation that they needed as much help as possible if they were going to catch a killer who was as shadowy as he was deadly. Thus, they utilized other experts, including forensic dentists who compared teeth with dental records, forensic anthropologists who specialized in skeletal remains, and forensic entomologists who understood how insect activity could be used to judge time of death.

They also consulted with experts on serial killers. One of these was Robert D. Keppel, who had been a member of the King County Police and one of the lead investigators in the Bundy case in Washington State in the 1970s. Keppel had pioneered many methods used to hunt serial killers and, after leaving the King County force, had worked on the Atlanta Child Murders in 1981.

Keppel reviewed the case in 1983, when the original task force had been working for only a few months. He studied procedures that were being followed and evidence that had been recovered. He then submitted a lengthy report containing recommendations for improvement. One of these recommendations highlighted the necessity of processing information more quickly and efficiently. Piles of papers—lab reports, tips, photos, and interviews—were piled everywhere in the task force office. Clues and important facts were being overlooked because of the confusion.

Thomas took Keppel's suggestions seriously. The task force had only one early Apple computer to work with, so he lobbied for two hundred thousand dollars in state money and a million-dollar grant to get an up-to-date computer system.

A map of locations of evidence compiled by the Green River task force in the 1980s.

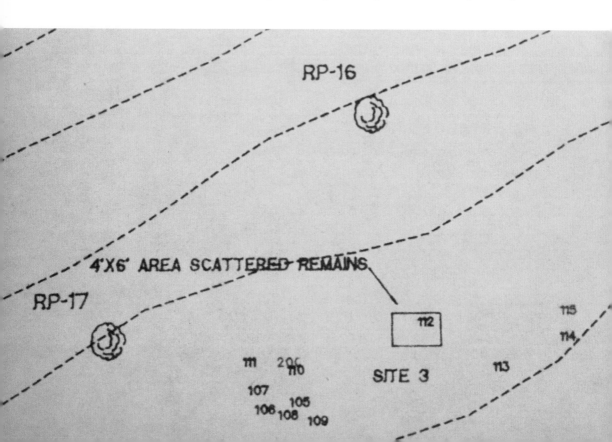

In 1984 the task force was upgraded from one early Apple computer, pictured, to an up-to-date computer system, which helped investigators work more efficiently.

After it was installed, clerks worked for two years to enter all the data into it. Once the data was accessible, investigators were able to make valuable connections that paid off later in the case.

The Ex-cop

The task force also sought advice from retired homicide detective Pierce Brooks, initiator and director of the Violent Criminal Apprehension Program (ViCAP), a nationwide computer system designed to track and correlate information on violent crime, particularly murder. Brooks had been a Los Angeles police officer for over twenty-five years, and he had worked on several high-profile murder cases in the United States.

Brooks came to Seattle in September 1985, reviewed the information that had been gathered over three years, and gave his impressions of the killer. Among other things, he believed the man might have been in the military in the past. Because he was so efficient at strangling, he might have been trained as a killer in the army's Special Forces. He was angry and hated women, but he did not come on strong with his victims at first. Control was important to him. He was secretive, hiding his victims. He had no interest in taunting the police as some killers did. He definitely had no compassion for the victims or remorse for what he was doing.

Brooks made one statement that seemed particularly significant to investigators. They had probably already interviewed the killer, but had not recognized him. "The odds are that his name is in [your records], probably more than once," Brooks said. "You just have to dig it out."[21]

The Profiler

Even before Brooks entered the case, task force leaders had turned to the Federal Bureau of Investigation for help in providing a profile of the killer. In September 1982 Special Agent John Douglas, who worked in the Bureau's Behavioral Science Unit in Quantico, Virginia, agreed to review the case and give them his conclusions.

Douglas was a psychologist who specialized in studying the criminal mind. At the time, he was one of three experts in the United States that studied crime scenes to gain information about the behavior, emotions, and motives of killers. Author Jon Zonderman writes, "[He was always trying to] get into the mind of the criminal and explore his (or her) thought processes in an attempt to tell investigators what kind of person would commit such a crime."[22]

Douglas's profile of the killer was twelve pages long. From his experience with other serial killers, he knew that the murderer had had violent fantasies from an early age. Perhaps he had been abused as a child. Certainly he came from a family where discord was common. He was likely to be Caucasian, in his mid-twenties to early thirties. He had an average or slightly above average intelligence but had had trouble in school and probably had dropped out. He possibly drank heavily and had trouble holding a steady job. Like other serial killers, he kept souvenirs from the victims and would be intensely interested in the investigation.

After studying specifics of the case, Douglas had additional insights. He believed only one man had carried out all the crimes. That man drove a conservative vehicle or vehicles, which were unlikely to be noticed. He had carried the victims, so he was in good physical condition. He had dumped his victims in a river that was good for fishing; therefore, he was likely an outdoorsman who was familiar with the river area.

Members of the Green River task force comb a hillside in Kent, Washington, looking for victims' remains.

Douglas believed the killer was confused in his feelings about women. He probably felt inadequate when it came to relationships and chose street prostitutes because he was not confident or charming enough to pick up a woman in a bar. He was drawn to women for sex but hated them enough to kill them. In a report to the FBI Douglas wrote, "He has felt that he has been 'burned' or 'lied to and fooled by women one too many times.' In his way of thinking, women are no good and cannot be trusted."[23] Killing was sexually gratifying to the murderer. It was a very personal act for him, something that he needed to do and took great satisfaction in doing well.

Douglas's final statement was a warning. "There is no burnout for this type of murderer. . . . He will not stop killing until he is caught."[24] The thought was alarming enough to make all members of the task force redouble their efforts on the case.

The FBI

John Douglas was not the only member of the FBI who helped with the Green River case. Agents based in Seattle had monitored the investigation from the beginning, ready to enter should any federal laws be violated. The FBI Crime Lab, located in Washington, D.C., was a valuable resource for the task force, too, not only for its skilled examiners but for its forensic and technical capabilities.

When bones of victims were found in Oregon on June 28, 1985, the FBI was able to become actively involved in the case. The killer had crossed state lines in committing his crimes, turning them into federal offenses. For several months after that, at least fourteen agents focused on possible suspects, and finally zeroed in on Ernest W. "Bill" McLean in early 1986. After questioning him extensively and giving him several polygraph tests, however, they had to admit that he was not their man. They then turned their attention to a suspect named Gary Ridgway, but he, too, was cleared.

By late 1986 federal agents were no closer to catching the killer than they had been a year earlier. Thus, they stepped back and let the task force resume the burden of the search. Task force members were not troubled by the agency's departure. As Reichert observes, "Many of our people had far more experience with violent crime and street-level investigation than most of the people the FBI sent to Seattle. . . . Add that we [the task force] had been up and running since the summer of 1982 . . . and you can see why we were . . . confident in our own abilities."[25]

Unconventional Sources

Although confident, the task force investigators sometimes accepted help from unconventional sources as they pursued the investigation. For instance, they sent informants to hypnotists to see if they could recall forgotten details of an incident. They allowed dowsers (people who find things in the ground with a divining rod) to try to locate bodies. They tolerated the presence of a psychic—a Kent, Washington, woman named Barbara Kubik-Patten—who claimed to experience visions that related to the victims.

Kubik-Patten first contacted the King County Police in 1982 and offered to use her abilities to help find the killer. Her services were rejected, but she remained on the fringes of the investigation, offering insights and advice. Then, in April 1984 she surprised skeptics by following one of her "visions" to a Green River victim who had been dumped along a service road off Interstate 90, east of Seattle. Reichert, who was not one of her fans, explains that the task force had been processing a newly discovered cluster of victims off I-90 when Kubik-Patten showed up. "On this day, we chased her away. She drove a couple of miles down the road, pulled over, and walked into the woods. There she spotted a . . . mostly decomposed body.

By the Numbers

$15 MILLION

Amount spent on the investigation by 1990

. . . We would identify her [the body] as Tina Marie Thompson, age twenty-two."[26]

Another unconventional contributor to the investigation was Bundy, the serial killer who was awaiting execution in Florida. In 1984 Bundy contacted the task force and insisted he could provide vital insights into the mind of "The Riverman," as he called the Green River Killer.

In December Reichert and Keppel flew to Florida to interview Bundy. They spent two days talking to him, learning how he thought and listening to his ideas. Bundy's suggestions were

Investigators carry a victim of the Green River Killer from the woods along Interstate 90, east of Seattle, Washington.

disappointing, however. The best of them involved holding a sex-slasher film festival where people are apparently killed on camera. According to Bundy, police could videotape those who attended, record their license plate numbers, and investigate them. "There's no better indicator of whether a man is capable of . . . killing all these women, than if he has that interest and goes out of his way to indulge that interest,"[27] he insisted. The investigators felt the suggestion was too expensive and involved too many legal complications for them to pursue it.

Somebody Knows Something

The task force even appealed to the public for help several times during the investigation. In November 1984 it worked with a local TV station to do a series of public service announcements, using the theme "Somebody Out There Knows Something." A one-hundred-thousand-dollar reward for information leading to an arrest was offered, and many tips came in. None led to the killer, however.

Four years later the task force helped reenact some elements of the Green River case for a television program, "Manhunt Live: A Chance to End the Nightmare." Television star Patrick Duffy acted as host and asked viewers to call a tip line, which was staffed by police officers and investigators. The show was an effort to jump-start the investigation, which was bogging down, but Reichert took the opportunity to speak directly to

Convicted murderer Ted Bundy, who gave suggestions to the task force as to how they might capture the Green River Killer.

In 1988 television star Patrick Duffy hosted the television program, "Manhunt Live: A Chance to End the Nightmare." Viewers were urged to call a tip line if they had information about the Green River murders.

the killer, too. "Many investigators believe you enjoy the killings. Several of us believe that you are haunted by them, that you want your own nightmare to stop. . . . If we identify you first, no one will care what you think or feel. It will be too late. Please call me."[28]

"Manhunt Live" was seen by over 50 million people, and more than fifteen hundred leads were generated. One helped police solve an unrelated murder. Another led them to a man who had escaped from police custody years before. The latter seemed promising because the offender fit the profile of the Green River Killer in every respect. As they began to investigate him, however, the task force investigators were cautious. Money, computers, expert advice, and four years of hard work had not brought the killer into their hands thus far. They wanted to believe they had reached the end of the case, but the possibility seemed almost too good to be true.

CHAPTER 3

The Suspects: So Many Possibilities

By the time "Manhunt Live" turned up a suspect in 1988, members of the task force had investigated thousands of men in their quest to find the killer. They had realized early on that the perpetrator was not a family friend or a disgruntled boyfriend but someone from the community who simply chose each woman at random and then moved on. That anonymity made him very hard to identify.

Even the best guide to his character, the FBI profile, was so general that it could be applied to thousands of men in the Northwest. The possibilities appeared endless and ranged from outdoorsmen to airline pilots. The staff of the *King County Journal* observed, "Everyone had a theory about the killer: a drifter, a loner, a hunter, a sadist, a rogue cop."[29]

Looking for Suspects

At first, investigators had few leads as they carried out their search for the killer. Because he was probably a familiar figure on the Strip, someone who regularly hired prostitutes, they first checked their files for men who had been arrested for soliciting in the past. Men who had assaulted or threatened women were of particular interest, because the killer could easily have progressed from assault to murder. The search yielded dozens of names, all of which had to be checked out. Crime writer Ann Rule writes, "The public . . . [had] no idea of how desperately hard they all worked, pounding pavements, making tens of thousands of phone calls, talking to people who told the truth, those who shaded the truth to suit themselves, and others who outright lied to them."[30]

As a second step, investigators again turned to people on the street. They asked if anyone had seen a victim getting into a car with a man just before she disappeared. They tried to establish what suspicious individuals looked like or what kinds of cars they drove. Many descriptions were given, but these ranged from thin men with long blond hair to stocky ones with dark curly hair. Vehicles potentially linked to the case ranged from taxis to pickups to vans.

Often the information investigators received was based on rumors, hearsay, and third-hand news that led them on searches that were as involved as they were time consuming. For instance, in 1982 investigators were told about a suspicious cab driver, Daniel Smith, who had allegedly talked about killing the women found in the Green River. When the facts were uncovered, however, it was discovered that a competitor of Smith, another cab driver named Melvyn Foster, had invented the story in order to get Smith in trouble.

Too Many Names

The task force soon compiled a list of several thousand "persons of interest." By 1986 there were almost one thousand "A" suspects alone—those who seemed like the best candidates—and only three hundred had been definitely ruled out. All these men had records of rape, assault, kidnapping, and other crimes of violence against women.

With so many men to focus on, it was quicker and easier to rule out the innocent than identify the guilty. Thus, the task force tried to prove that a suspect could not have done the crimes. For instance, early in the case a young woman accused a prominent Seattle sportscaster of being the killer, claiming he had tried to choke her while they were having sex. The man admitted the incident but denied any other guilt. His work records, provided by his employer, proved that he had been at a television station when most of the girls went missing, and so he could not have committed the crimes.

"Green River Gary"

Gary Ridgway was only one of many suspects in the Green River investigation. As author Ann Rule relates in Green River, Running Red, *Ridgway's low IQ and habit of making mistakes made him the butt of jokes at Kenworth, where he painted trucks for a living.*

Gary Ridgway had always been proud of his job with Kenworth and the image he had there, or believed he had there. He was a dependable, punctual employee, and he usually managed to follow the computer instructions provided to mix the paint that stylized the big rigs. But sometimes his dyslexia made it difficult for him to remember the numbers on the computers associated with specialty paint jobs. On a bad day, he might ruin a couple of jobs by getting mixed up on a three-color trim, and then he raged at himself. One day he "ruined several trucks" because he got the sequences mixed up. He even had one three-day period when he added the wrong chemicals to the paint. Worst of all, he occasionally painted the wrong truck entirely. The bosses always let him do it over, and he did without protest. One of his nicknames around the plant was "Wrong-Way" and he hated that. But he couldn't show his anger at work because he feared being fired. . . .

After the task force investigators searched his locker [in 1987], Ridgway got another nickname at work. . . . Nobody really thought he was capable of killing more than three dozen prostitutes, but there was the similarity of his initials that begged for jokes at his expense: "G.R." for Gary Ridgway, and "G.R." for Green River. He soon became "Green River Gary" at Kenworth.

Ann Rule, *Green River, Running Red.* New York: Free Press, 2004, p. 293.

Like the sportscaster, many suspects in the Green River case were guilty of assaulting prostitutes but could not have been the killer. Some suspects, such as John Norris Hanks, who was linked to the murder of five San Francisco women between 1972 and 1978, were currently in prison. Others were less-hardened criminals. A well-to-do farmer in the Kent area was investigated but eliminated after he held a prostitute captive in his barn for a week before letting her go. A marine veteran was eliminated although he had kidnapped a young prostitute, tied her up in his van, and threatened to kill her. Both men were arrested for their crimes, however.

The Cab Driver

While many suspects were quickly eliminated, others remained under suspicion for a considerable period of time. Cab driver Melvin Foster was the first of these. He came to the task force's attention in 1982. Reichert notes, "With his talk on the street and adamant statements about Dan Smith, Melvyn Foster was a little too interested in the Green River case and a little too eager to help us pin the murders on Smith."[31]

Foster had driven cabs in Seattle and on the Strip for years, and he claimed to have a deep concern for young prostitutes and runaways. His personality and his actions combined to stir up serious suspicions in the investigators, however. He was odd, offbeat, and talked too much. He bragged and exaggerated. He portrayed himself as a superhero but was in fact thin, wore glasses, and had thinning hair. He had also been arrested and served two separate prison terms for auto theft.

Foster fit the FBI profile for the killer, and at least once he came into headquarters to offer information, proving that he was interested in the case. He was caught in a lie, too. When shown photos of the dead girls, he denied knowing them. Later he changed his story and admitted that he did. "I've never made a secret of having been acquainted with a few of them (the victims)," he stated. "Cab drivers meet the seedy side of life if you drive around town."[32]

Convinced he was hiding something, in September 1982 investigators invited Foster to headquarters and interrogated him for hours. They knew that long interviews wore down suspects' defenses, causing them to confess if they were guilty. Foster revealed bits of information that could be incriminating, such as the fact that he often spent the night in Seattle rather than making the drive to his home in Lacey, Washington, 50 miles (89km) south of the city. He insisted that he was innocent, however. Finally, detectives asked him to take a polygraph test. Foster agreed, but did not pass. This aroused everyone's suspicions still further.

"Lay an Egg, or Get off the Nest"

When Foster failed the polygraph, investigators asked permission to search his home and car. He agreed. Reichert notes:

> I had hoped that we might find incriminating photos or a collection of items taken from the victims. Many serial killers have accumulated such 'souvenirs' as trophies or reminders of their crimes. We found none of these items but . . . in the car we found . . . photos of nude women and some pubic hairs, which Melvyn said must be linked to a friend who had borrowed the car.[33]

Investigators still had no proof that Foster was the killer, but they remained suspicious. They asked him to provide hair and blood samples. Foster agreed. Analysis of deoxyribonucleic acid (DNA), genetic material found in body fluids, was not available at the time, but other tests carried out in the lab could indicate whether the samples were similar to those found

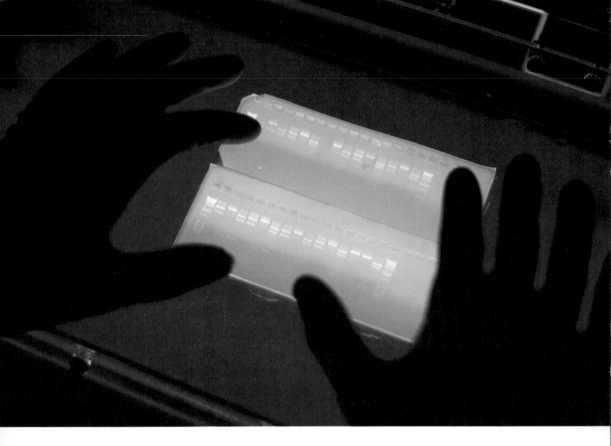

on the victims. Foster and his home were also placed under twenty-four-hour surveillance.

The continued attention finally made Foster angry. He began trying to shake off detectives who tailed him. He complained of police harassment. He contacted Seattle television and newspaper reporters and announced that he was being investigated as a suspect in the Green River case. He gave the press his version of the story and threatened to sue the task force. "I feel like the basic rights of a citizen have been trampled on," he said, demanding that investigators either arrest him or leave him alone. "Lay an egg or get off the nest,"[34] was the way he put it.

The investigators did not comply. However, as prostitutes continued to disappear and more bodies were found, they wondered how Foster could be murdering them while he was always under their eye. Even Reichert, who had been convinced that Foster was their man, had to admit by late 1983, "We had been watching Foster so closely that I had to doubt he was

Serving a Search Warrant

When police officers convince a judge that they have reason to believe that criminal activity is occurring at a private locale, the judge issues a search warrant, allowing them to enter those premises. Officers must follow correct procedure when they serve and execute the warrant, however. That procedure is as follows:

1 **Knock and announce:** The officer who is serving the warrant knocks on the door of the house or business to be entered and announces his purpose in wanting to enter. If no one is present, he posts a copy of the warrant in a visible place and the search team enters.

2 **Search and seizure:** Police search the building and confiscate the evidence they are looking for. The search and seizure must be limited to specific objects and places named in the warrant. Other items, rooms, outbuildings, and vehicles require a separate search warrant. The officer collecting evidence under the warrant must provide a receipt and inventory for the property taken.

3 **Arrest:** If police determine a crime has been committed, they can take into custody those they suspect of committing the crime.

4 **Miranda warning:** Police must read suspects in custody a Miranda warning before asking guilt-seeking questions. Suspects must be clearly informed that they have the right to remain silent, and that anything they say will be used against them in court; that they have the right to consult with an attorney and have that attorney present during interrogation; and that if they cannot afford an attorney, one will be provided at no cost.

responsible for these disappearances. This highlighted the chilling possibility that the Green River killer was quietly continuing his depraved activities safely out of our view."[35]

The Outdoorsman

As the task force's interest in Foster waned, FBI agents on the case in 1985 focused on Bill McLean, who was a construction worker living near the airport and also an avid outdoorsman. McLean was extremely strong and athletic. He enjoyed trapping animals, had detailed maps of the Washington backwoods, and was known to frequent the exact areas where bodies had been found. He owned handcuffs, a police badge, and a red bubble light similar to those once found on police cars. The task force had long suspected that the killer sometimes posed as a police officer in order to lure prostitutes into his car, so McLean's possession of police equipment was significant.

McLean did not patronize prostitutes, and he had been arrested only once in the past, and that had been for burglary. But when people who knew him were interviewed, they told the FBI of some bizarre behavior. For instance, McLean had allegedly mentioned wanting to pick up a prostitute and kill her. He apparently kept a mannequin in the back of his truck and slashed at it with knives.

McLean looked very suspicious. But because there was no hard evidence on which to arrest him, in early 1986 the FBI decided they would have to pressure him into admitting his crimes. On February 6 they put a plan into action. McLean and his wife were picked up and taken to headquarters, while FBI and task force members searched the couple's home, McLean's parents' house, and his numerous vehicles. The press learned of the search and filled McLean's neighborhood with lights, cameras, and reporters. The next morning many broadcast the news that McLean was being investigated in connection with the Green River killings. The *Seattle Post-Intelligencer* newspaper quoted an unnamed police source as saying, "There is an awfully lot that looks good. There's an awful lot of good probable cause [evidence]."[36]

Although the press branded McLean guilty, investigators who interrogated him were beginning to have their doubts. Not only did McLean insist that he was innocent, but his demeanor and his reactions when confronted with items of evidence told them he was not the killer. Their doubts were strengthened when McLean passed five lie detector tests. No hair, fiber, blood, or any other hard evidence that linked him to the Green River killings were found in his home or car, either. On February 7 they released him and announced to the press that he was not their man.

The incident did nothing for anyone's reputation. The public and King County officials blamed the mistake on task force incompetence. McLean himself filed multimillion-dollar lawsuits against King County, the task force, and five news agencies, claiming they had humiliated and ridiculed him and his wife, as well as violated their privacy. The suit was settled and McLean was awarded thirty thousand dollars in 1989. By then the task force had removed his name from its list of suspects and was focusing on other possibilities.

The Green River Task Force relied on polygraph machines, which measure perspiration, respiration, and heart rate, to help determine if a suspect was lying.

The Truck Painter

In the continual quest to identify the killer, one of the better possibilities seemed to be a suspect named Gary Ridgway. Ridgway was a truck painter who was a frequent customer of prostitutes on the Strip. In May 1984 he contacted the task force, telling investigators that he had met Nelson—one of the victims—in 1983. The fact that he had initated contact caught their attention. When asked to take a polygraph test, however, Ridgway agreed and passed.

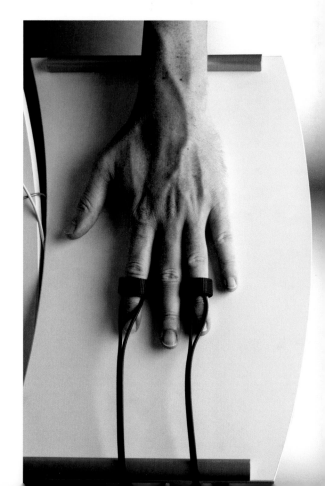

In 1985 detective Matthew Haney joined the task force, reviewed the list of suspects, and decided to take another look at Ridgway. Over the course of the next two years Haney gathered a pile of what appeared to be extremely damaging facts. Computer records showed that Ridgway had been accused of choking a prostitute near the SeaTac airport in 1980. Port of Seattle police had investigated the incident (SeaTac airport is managed by the Port of Seattle), and Ridgway had explained that he had assaulted the woman because she had bitten him and made him angry.

In February 1983 Port of Seattle police had again interviewed Ridgway when they found him parked in a car with a prostitute near the airport. The prostitute was McGinness,

In 1987 investigators tested hair, saliva, and blood samples, which were provided by suspect Gary Ridgway. No hard evidence tied him to the case at the time.

who disappeared four months later. In April 1983 it had been Ridgway's truck that Robert Woods identified after the disappearance of Malvar. This meant that he had been connected in one way or another with three of the missing women—Nelson, McGinness, and Malvar.

More incriminating facts surfaced in 1986 when Haney located and interviewed Ridgway's ex-wife, Marcia. Marcia admitted that Ridgway had once tried to choke her. She stated, "I was a little drunk and I got out of our van and stumbled. I started to reach for the door and the next thing I knew he had his hands around my neck and he was choking me from behind. I started fighting him. He finally let go."[37]

Interested, Haney asked Marcia to show him places that she and Ridgway had frequented on outings such as picnics and hikes during the years they had been married between 1973 and 1981. Almost all the sites Marcia pointed out were near recovery sites. For instance, she and Ridgway had picked apples and blackberries around the empty lots close to the airport. They had ridden inner tubes in the snow at a recovery site on I-90.

Haney next obtained Ridgway's work records, which showed that he had never been at work when victims disappeared. In addition, Ridgway had been on strike for three weeks in 1983 when the killer had been exceptionally active. Three women had been killed during that period.

With a gut feeling that he had found the killer, Haney obtained a warrant to search Ridgway's home and car in April 1987. Investigators made a thorough search for hair, fibers, or anything belonging to one of the women, with no results. Ridgway refused to take another lie detector test but did provide hair, saliva, and blood samples.

By the Numbers

4,100

Number of suspects investigated by 1986

Ridgway looked like the best suspect they had, but all the evidence against him was circumstancial or indirect. No fingerprints, hair, fiber, or anything else directly tied him to the case. The task force investigators feared that if they arrested him without enough evidence, a jury might acquit him. Then, if more evidence were uncovered later, proving without a doubt that he was the killer, he could never be tried again because of the double jeopardy law. They resolved to send his hair and saliva samples to the crime lab, keep him on their list, and see what happened in the future.

The Law Student

Even though Ridgway appeared to be their man, the task force members did not stop investigating other suspicious individuals. They had seen many good suspects cleared in the past, and they did not want to miss the real killer through overconfidence. Thus, when law student William J. Stevens II came to their attention in 1989, they checked him out as thoroughly as they had every other person of interest.

Stevens was arrested in Spokane, Washington, in January 1989 as a result of tips generated by the TV program "Manhunt Live: A Chance to End the Nightmare." Tipsters said Stevens talked a great deal about Bundy, as well as the Green River case. He hated prostitutes and claimed to have been involved in their torture. When arrested, though, Stevens immediately issued a statement in his own defense. "I am not the Green River killer. They have made me out to be a very bad person, and I am not."[38]

Stevens was too suspicious to ignore, however. When police searched the home in which he had been living, they found multiple driver licenses issued to him under different names. They found dozens of guns and photos of nude women, some of them Spokane-area prostitutes. He also had police badges, surveillance equipment, license plates issued to police vehicles, and an old police car, which he had fitted up with a police radio, a radar unit, and blue emergency lights.

He could easily have lured his victims into his car by posing as a policeman.

Not only did Stevens possess suspicious items, he was a wanted man. He had been convicted of burglary in 1979 while he was a student at the University of Washington in Seattle. Two years later he had escaped from a King County work release program and disappeared. He had lived in the Portland area until May 1985, when he moved back to Spokane to attend Gonzaga University School of Law. Between 1981 and 1985 he had regularly traveled between Spokane, Seattle, and Portland. "Records obtained thus far have failed to provide him with an alibi for any of the . . . suspected Green River homicides," stated new task force commander Robert Evans in July 1989. "Instead, interviews and records have produced . . . facts that tend to establish that Stevens is a viable suspect in the Green River homicides, and possibly others in the Pacific Northwest."[39]

The faces of the Green River victims haunted investigators like task force member Dan Nolan.

A closer check of Stevens's history proved otherwise, however. Investigators learned that on dates in 1982 and 1983 when the killer was active, Stevens could be placed in another part of the country. By October 1989 everyone had to conclude that he was not the man for whom they were looking. "It took us a long time to contact all the people we needed to as a result of information we gathered through the investigation," said Evans. "But as we did that and the timeline of his whereabouts became more complete, we could no longer in good conscience leave him as a viable suspect."[40]

Stevens was cleared just months before the Green River Task Force was disbanded in June 1990. Despite dedication and hard work, its members had not been successful in catching the killer, and the public had become convinced that a successful outcome was impossible. Reichert wrote, "Many people have an unrealistic view of police work. They believe that we can solve any crime if we only try hard enough. . . . [But] nothing is harder than finding a bad guy who attacks strangers and knows how to hide his tracks."[41]

CHAPTER 4

The Obstacles: The Case Bogs Down

Determining the guilt or innocence of an array of devious suspects was just one challenge the Green River Task Force faced throughout its twenty-year investigation. It was plagued by other problems, too, that ranged from inexperience to a lack of public support. "I am [not] abdicating from any mistakes that were made during my involvement," said Kraske, who received his share of blame for not solving the case. "It's just that it would have made things a little less difficult if you had known that you had the support these investigations demanded."[42]

The most serious hurdle to be overcome was the fact that no one foresaw how large and complex the case was going to become. Valuable time was lost while everyone came to terms with the notion that extraordinary measures would be needed to solve it. "We were confident that the whole thing would be over in a few months," recalled one of the original task force members. "None of us believed it would take any longer than that. We all thought we'd have the guy in jail and that we'd all be back doing what we were supposed to be doing before anyone realized we were gone. . . .

We were *wrong*."[43]

A Slow Start

In the early 1980s when the killer was most active, the task force was most plagued by its own inexperience. Those detectives who had worked the Bundy murders had moved on to other jobs, leaving behind men and women who had never worked a serial murder case before. In 1982, for instance, Reichert, the lead investigator, was thirty-two years old and

Dave Reichert and other task force members felt deep compassion for families who lost someone to the Green River Killer.

had been in the county's major crimes unit less than two years. His partner, Bob Moria, also had little homicide experience. One of their colleagues, Sue Peters, was twenty-four and a new hire of the King County Police. Spokeswoman Fae Brooks had worked the sex crimes unit investigating sexual assaults and had sometimes acted as a police artist.

Because of their inexperience, they sometimes made mistakes. When Coffield and Bonner's bodies were found in the Green River within less than a month of each other, for instance, no one considered that the deaths might be connected or that a serial killer might be operating in the region. After processing the Bonner crime scene, no surveillance was set up in the area in case the killer returned. As a result, when the killer dumped the next three bodies in the same region in the next few weeks, no one spotted him.

Other departmental deficiencies added to task force shortcomings. In the first months when most of the killings took place, the King County Police continued to largely ignore the many missing person reports that came in. A new report was commonly put on the bottom of a pile of pending cases, and

the top report was filed. Thus, even when a prostitute was reported missing, no one notified the task force of her disappearance. Sometimes the discovery and identification of her
bones were the first clues that she had disappeared.

Because of danger from the killer, the vice division also dis-
continued "prostitution decoys"—female police officers who
posed as prostitutes in order to arrest male customers. No one
wanted to risk the life of a police officer. This was the time
when the killer was most active, however, and such operations
might have helped identify him.

Resentment and Division

A lack of support from other law enforcement officers made
the task force's job harder, too. Even King County detectives
who were not chosen to be part of the expanded task force in
1984 were sometimes slow to offer help when asked. Their
stance was often due to anger over being overlooked for the
prestigious position. Sometimes it was because they had to cope
with less manpower and funds, while the task force seemed
to have the best of everything. Guillen and Smith observe:

> Uniform patrol officers came to view their Green River
> colleagues as secretive and clannish. The whole precinct
> seemed to be run for their benefit. Ordinary cops had
> to wait in line for the copy machine. . . . The Green
> River people got all the best parking spaces. The feel-
> ing of separation was worsened when one of Adamson's
> lieutenants, to build morale, ordered special green ny-
> lon windbreakers clearly labeled Green River Task Force
> for all the task force members. The new jackets did the
> job . . . but contributed further to the alienation."[44]

Members of the vice department resented the task force
because it was involved in their jurisdiction—prostitution and
the Strip. They supported the investigation, but not as whole-
heartedly as they might have. For instance, while the task force

Frustrated and Angry

The Green River Killer murdered prostitutes, but these young women were not his only victims. In his book Chasing the Devil, *Dave Reichert describes the anger and frustration parents felt as they tried to cope with the situation.*

No one was more upset by the mystery of the Green River killings than those parents who had reported their daughters missing months and even years ago. We heard from some of these mothers and fathers almost every week. Others, like Mertie Winston, tried to restrain themselves. Mertie didn't want to bother me, so she saved up her questions until she couldn't bear it anymore and then called me to go down the list.

"Why haven't you caught him?"

"Do you have any evidence at all?"

"Why is this so hard for you to do?"

Sometimes I could share information with Mertie, and sometimes what I knew had to be kept secret. Many parents, Mertie included, had theories about the killer. She would focus on someone and push us to investigate. When the lead didn't pan out, she would get frustrated and then angry. Later, though, she'd bring cookies to the task force office.

It was often hard to tell whether these parents believed their daughters were alive or had concluded they were dead. Either way, they needed some sort of physical evidence before they could even think about trying to return to their normal lives. Like us, they both dreaded and welcomed the news that a body had been discovered. I would visit or call them as soon as I could share anything about the identity of new remains.

David Reichert, *Chasing the Devil.* New York: Little, Brown , 2004, p. 134.

was trying to win prostitutes' confidence, vice officers continued to arrest them for prostitution. The women were thus wary of talking freely for fear they or their friends would get into trouble. After an arrest, vice officers did not interview prostitutes to see if they knew anything about the killer. Neither did they go out of their way to write down license plates of men who solicited prostitutes on the Strip.

Poor communication between the task force and outside police departments at times slowed the investigation, too. Sometimes this situation was unintentional. For instance, the Des Moines police did not immediately pass on information regarding Marie Malvar getting into the pickup truck with the primer spot because they had not been told Malvar was a prostitute. Therefore, they did not immediately think of sending a report to the task force regarding her disappearance.

Family members like Jose Malvar Jr., brother of victim Marie Malvar, became impatient with authorities when the Green River Killer was not quickly apprehended.

Sometimes the poor communication was based on a police department's reluctance to believe that the killer was responsible for crimes in its area. When bodies of prostitutes were found near Portland, Oregon, beginning in the fall of 1984, for instance, Portland police initially refused to cooperate with the task force. Eventually it was determined that some of the Oregon victims had fallen prey to other men, but Denise Bush and Shirley Sherrill, found outside Portland in June 1985, were Green River victims. As Reichert noted, "It was a good thing we cleared the air with authorities in Portland. . . . If Denise and Shirley had been reported as missing persons in Portland, they would have been assumed to be victims of a local crime. But they had disappeared from King County."[45]

Information Backlog

Another obstacle to catching the killer was the massive amount of information and evidence that the task force had to process. Normally, material gathered in a murder case could be contained in a three-ring binder. By the end of the first year alone the task force had filled fifteen binders. "[We were] overwhelmed with information," Adamson recalls, noting that the task force tried hard to stay organized. "We redesigned the case file books so we could find things easily. We got the physical evidence together. We had one room with case binders listing the Missing, the Homicides, and the Physical Evidence."[46]

Evidence that needed to be examined microscopically had to be sent to the Washington State Patrol crime lab. Kraske noted one year into the investigation: "We've put about seven hundred and twenty different items of evidence into the crime lab for analysis. That includes body hair, soil samples, all kinds of things."[47] In many cases, one piece of evidence yielded dozens of clues. For instance, when a shirt or a pair of socks was processed, every bit of dust, dirt, fiber, and hair that was brushed off the garment had to be examined under a microscope as well.

The mass of material created a backlog in the lab and forced investigators to wait long periods for results. It also pressured

lab workers to get results as quickly as possible. In at least one case, evidence was not as exhaustively analyzed as it might have been. Tiny specks of red, brown, and metallic blue paint had been found on some of the first victims' clothing, and lab technicians had compared the specks with a variety of known paint samples. They could not make a match, however. The samples were not sent to forensic microscopist Skip Palenik, however, who was teaching classes at the Washington crime lab in the 1980s and would have been able to identify them. In 2002, when Palenik finally analyzed the samples at his Microtrace Laboratory in Elgin, Illinois, he was able to determine that the paint was an expensive brand made by DuPont, used in small amounts when painting trucks. "Had I looked at the stuff in the '80s, . . . it would have been a great investigative lead,"[48] he stated.

The Green River murders produced massive amounts of information and evidence that the task force had to process. By the end of the first year alone the task force had filled fifteen binders.

Suggestions and Confessions

In addition to coping with inexperience, lack of support, and a backlog of evidence, the task force had to deal with interruptions from members of the public who believed they had identified the killer. Letters and calls came in regularly. Investigators even received them at home. Although sincere, many of the suggestions were bizarre and improbable. For instance, one anonymous letter writer claimed the killer was the director of a renowned symphony orchestra. In another instance, a Washington, D.C., lawyer claimed the killer was a retarded person who lived in the basement of his apartment house. An amateur detective from Tacoma calling himself "Agent X-2" insisted that the killer was simply a robber intent on stealing prostitutes' jewelry. Investigators only had to stake out pawnshops and they would catch him. While the most outrageous suggestions were ignored, many of them warranted investiga-

Serial killer Henry Lee Lucas was one of several men who falsely confessed to the Green River murders.

tion, and this added to the already enor-mous workload the task force faced.

There were also numerous individuals who wasted the task force's time by false-ly confessing to the killings. For instance, in 1983 serial killer Henry Lee Lucas, in prison in Texas, told authorities that he had committed the Green River murders. His claim seemed unlikely. He had been judged mentally disturbed and was inclined to confess to any murder that was brought to his attention. Nevertheless, investiga-tors had to rule him out. They eventually determined that he had not been in the Pacific Northwest at the time of the Green River murders.

In 1984 the *San Francisco Chronicle* newspaper carried the confessions of two violent offenders, Richard Carbone and Robert Matthias, imprisoned in San Francisco County. The men claimed to have worked together to commit the Green River murders. One stated, "Do I think I am the one they are looking for? I would have to say yes."[49]

When a task force detective went to San Francisco to check their story and prior prison records, however, he found that the men had been locked up in California during the time most of the murders were taking place in 1982 and 1983.

Media Interference

As the story published by the *San Francisco Chronicle* demon-strated, the press helped complicate life for the task force. After the bodies of Chapman, Hinds, and Mills were found in August 1982, for instance, newspersons broadcast the fact that police were staking out the Green River in hopes of catching the killer, should he return. No one could say for sure if the killer watched the broadcast, but he never deposited bodies in that vicinity again.

Complications were created by newspersons on the Strip after the first reports of the killings came out in 1982. Reporters

Becoming a Forensic Scientist

Job Description:

Forensic scientists perform routine analysis on physical evidence in criminal cases submitted to the forensic laboratory. They also interpret analytical results, prepare written opinion reports, and may testify as expert witnesses in courts of law. Although the work is mainly laboratory based, there is the possibility of visits to crime scenes, which may involve exposure to unpleasant situations.

Education:

A bachelor of science degree in forensic science, natural science, or a closely related field is required. Those interested in working with DNA must complete at least one undergraduate or graduate level course in each of the following subjects: biochemistry, genetics, and molecular biology.

Qualifications:

An aspiring forensic scientist should have a logical and analytical approach to work; have highly developed observational and scientific skills; understand legal issues and the application of testing techniques; remain objective while reaching critical conclusions; have strong written and verbal communication skills; and perform well within a team, often to tight deadlines.

Salary:

A forensic scientist can earn a salary that ranges from $36,000 to more than $60,000 annually.

were more numerous than police as they interviewed anyone who would speak to them, looking for a story. They speculated on what they heard and then asked interviewees to comment on the speculations. The rumor and guesswork were taken by many of their audience as fact, and investigators soon discovered that witnesses' memories were influenced by such input. For instance, the *Seattle Times* newspaper reported that the first women to be murdered might have known each other, and, shortly thereafter, informants were telling the police that they had heard that all the victims knew each other. Investigators could not be sure the information was accurate, because they did not know if their sources had gotten it from the *Seattle Times* or from their own knowledge. Reichert writes, "We could never be sure whether a witness was relaying an actual experience or a tale blended with facts from TV broadcasts and newspaper articles."[50]

In their efforts to get new facts more quickly than their competitors, newspeople always hurried to the scene after a body was discovered. Investigators had to be on the watch to keep them from contaminating the area and snapping photos of the remains. They interrogated task force spokespersons, hoping for information even when there was none to give. At all times they listened for subtle hints and watched body language. If an investigator smiled and appeared relaxed, they postulated that a break in the case was coming. If he looked serious, they guessed that investigators were discouraged.

When the task force failed to catch the killer in a few months, the media became openly critical of its progress. In August 1984 the *Seattle Times* concluded that Kraske, the former task force leader, and Bernard Winckoski, the former sheriff, were to blame because the killer had not been caught. In 1987 the *Seattle Times* ran a weeklong series on the Green River investigation. Each installment carried the heading "Green River, What Went Wrong?" with subheadings such as "Valuable Time Lost," and "Investigation Gaps." In 1989 the *Seattle Times* published an editorial cartoon that dubbed the task force the "Green River Task Farce." Already sensitive to their failure to catch the killer, investigators were angry and resentful of the criticism. Reichert observed, "We were being subjected to unrealistic expectations, and hindsight made it seem as if we had operated like a bunch of bumbling idiots."[51]

Lack of Public Interest

The press helped tarnish the task force's image with the public, but that public was already somewhat detached from the case even before that happened. As in early 1984, when a large number of bodies were being found, only four people turned out for a King County–sponsored community meeting designed to share information and ease concerns about the murders.

Apathy and disillusionment continued to grow over time. Few King County residents believed the killer would ever be caught, but most remained unconcerned about that fact. This was because they did not fear that he would target them. They knew that he went after prostitutes, who were seen as the "throwaways" of society. In fact, they believed, he did not pose a threat to ordinary citizens.

Only a few people—most of them women—were outspokenly critical of the lack of progress. In March 1984 a San Francisco–based radical feminist group, the U.S. Prostitutes Collective, verbally attacked the police for not catching the killer. Spokeswoman Rachel West complained, "The investigation by the police has been too slow. Money is being wasted. I don't think they're taking women's lives seriously."[52]

That same winter the Seattle-based Women's Coalition to Stop the Green River Murders gave voice to criticisms, too. Four hundred women, many of them mothers of the victims, marched through downtown Seattle carrying candles, then rallied at the courthouse where they lashed out at authorities. "If fifty-two white, middle-class, college girls were missing or dead there would be an entirely different response,"[53] said Cookie Hunt, a speaker at the rally, citing the number of women that the *Seattle Times* believed might be dead and missing.

These groups were not mainstream organizations, however, so their protests were largely ignored. The task force understood the anger, but did not appreciate the criticism. Team members knew that the case had occupied their every waking moment for years. They could do little, however, when King County leaders listened to mainstream voters who wanted the police to put their time and money into other community issues and let the Green River case remain unsolved.

Money Problems

Faced with critical media and faint public interest, the task force had to fight for financial support both at the beginning and the end of the investigation. When the first task force was formed in 1982, King County executive Randy Revelle believed that ten thousand dollars would be adequate to work the case. Kraske, who did not believe in challenging authority, made do with what he was allotted rather than fight for more. As a result, by December 1983, when he was transferred to another precinct, money had run out, most of the original task force had been assigned to other tasks, and the investigation was stalled.

The investigation lacked a dynamic leader until Vernon Thomas became sheriff in April 1983. Thomas immediately made the case for enlarging the task force budget but was slowed by the King County council and others who were skeptical that more money would make any difference in the case. They wondered if the killer was still out there. If so, they were skeptical that he could ever be caught. They had heard that if an offender was not caught within the first forty-eight hours of committing the crime, the chances of getting him were cut in half.

Thomas was able to convince them otherwise and got increased funding for more officers and equipment. He faced serious opposition again in 1985, however, when Revelle was defeated by Tim Hill, a cost-conscious politician who believed that task force money would be better used combating King County's growing drug and crime problems. The public agreed. Thus, beginning in 1986 the task force's budget was cut. Some task force detectives were

By the Numbers

48

Number of murders the Green River Killer admitted to carrying out

transferred to other departments. Fewer detectives meant a slower and less efficient investigation. Judy DeLeon, mother of victim Carrie Rois, was angry at the moves. "It makes me and some of the other parents feel like the deaths of our daughters aren't important to anybody. It's bad enough that this happened. But now it's like the King County executive is saying, 'Well, that's too bad, but now we're going to do something else.'"[54]

By November 1986 even the most dedicated members of the task force realized that it was being phased out. A frustrated and discouraged Adamson, who had managed the investigation since Kraske's departure, moved on to another job. In December 1987 Thomas resigned after years of fighting Hill's budget cuts. Key players, including Reichert and Brooks, transferred to other positions between 1988 and 1990. Ann Rule writes, "A tremendous amount of work and dedication hadn't brought the real killer to his knees. Some of the best detectives in America had stepped up to the plate, full of energy and confidence, and struck out."[55]

King County sheriff Dave Reichert, left, speaks to former sheriff Vern Thomas in November 2003. Thomas was the sheriff when the murders surfaced in 1982, and Reichert was the lead detective.

Waiting and Wondering

Budget cuts brought the Green River investigation to a virtual close in 1991. By that year, Tom Jensen, who had joined the case in 1984, was the only full-time member of the task force. The staff of the *King County Journal* observed,

> Jenson spent most of his time alone, tediously calling up lists of names and bytes of evidence on his computer screen, seeking correlations. The telephone would ring at least once each day. The tips were usually bogus; the caller on the other end of the line was usually someone obsessed with the case. Still, Jensen listened to all of them, because it would take just one good tip to catch the killer.[56]

The case had helped bring change to King County. By 1991 the Strip had become less crime ridden. Some of the many drug dealers and prostitutes had moved away as more police patrolled the streets and new businesses opened. Rent-by-the-hour motels had been modernized and now catered to families.

The King County Police Department had grown in sophistication. Its resources included a modern computer system, a computerized fingerprint processor, laser-based fingerprint and fiber detection analyzers, and high-tech surveillance equipment. Police departments across the nation consulted with it when dealing with serial killers and sexual predators.

None of that entirely made up for the fact that the Green River Killer remained at large. As Smith and Guillen write, "Skeletons and bodies continued to appear in the woods. . . . The families of the missing continued to wait, while the families of the dead were left to wonder: Would the Green River murders ever be solved? Would the dead finally become a mere footnote to history?"[57]

CHAPTER 5

Arrest and Confession: The Mind of a Killer

As the 1990s progressed, the Green River Killer case faded from the public view. Remains were still discovered periodically, but they were from earlier disappearances. Contrary to the predictions of the experts, the murderer, whoever he was, seemed to have stopped killing. Even the most dedicated law officer had to admit that the case was cold.

Then, in 1997 Dave Reichert became King County sheriff. Although he had not worked the case for ten years, he had not forgotten the pain the victims' families had suffered. He resolved to make another try to catch the killer. "When I became sheriff, the victims' families and others hoped that I would do something to solve the mystery," he remembers. "I hoped I could make some progress, too, but I knew it wouldn't be easy."[58]

Breakthrough!

In April 2001 Reichert chose a team to reinvestigate the killings. Headed by Bruce Kalin, the team included other original members of the investigation—James Doyon and Randy Mullinax, as well as Haney and Jensen. Upon taking the job, Kalin said, "Our first order of business will be to continue our investigation of the Ridgway case. . . . Obviously, I feel a sense of responsibility not only to the former commanders, but to the surviving friends and family of the victims. . . . This has always been a quest for fact and truth."[59]

As the team reviewed the case, Reichert encouraged Jensen to send biological evidence taken from several victims and suspects for retesting using the latest DNA technology. In 1988

Jensen had sent samples to one of the few DNA laboratories then in existence in the United States, but genetic material from the victims was too deteriorated to get accurate results. As DNA technology evolved, however, even degraded samples could be successfully analyzed and compared to a known sample. There was a good chance that matches could be made if the evidence was resubmitted.

In the summer of 2001 Jensen resubmitted his samples to the Washington State Patrol crime lab, which had just obtained the equipment, personnel, and training necessary to carry out the latest DNA procedures. These included a method called polymerase chain reaction–short tandem repeats (PCR-STR), wherein a small amount of DNA is reproduced in order to get enough for testing.

A scientist works with DNA equipment. Investigators in the Green River case successfully matched DNA found on some victims' bodies to Ridgway.

Detectives search for evidence in the backyard of the home of Gary Ridgway on December 3, 2001.

In September Jensen had results, and they were significant. DNA found on Mills and Hinds was definitively linked to one of the known suspects in the case—truck painter Ridgway. Reichert remembers how he reacted when Jensen brought him the news. "Tears began to flood my eyes, and my throat closed a bit with emotion. I could see that Tom was on the brink of tears, too. As much as we always expected to solve the case, neither of us was quite prepared. Now we knew we could charge Ridgway with the murders of all three victims found at the river on August 15, 1982."[60]

The Arrest

The task force would have liked to arrest Ridgway immediately but decided to organize the evidence first in order to have the strongest case possible. Working in secret so the media would not get the story, the task force reviewed the evidence and helped King County prosecutors write up the charges. The lab soon successfully matched DNA found on Christensen's body to Ridgway, so that murder charge was added as well.

While all that was going on, investigators established round-the-clock surveillance on Ridgway, who was still living in the area with his third wife, Judith. The surveillance revealed that their suspect continued to drive along the Strip, and on November 16 he was arrested by a vice cop for soliciting a prostitute. The possibility that he might kill again was on everyone's mind. Reichert observes, "Obviously he was out trolling again. We would have to pick him up as soon as possible. The task force team worked day and night to allow us to grab him ahead of schedule."[61]

The arrest was made on November 30, 2001. As Ridgway was getting into his truck, preparing to leave work at 3:00 P.M., detectives surrounded him and told him he was under arrest for the murders of Hinds, Chapman, Mills, and Christensen. Ridgway did not seem surprised and went quietly. Reichert announced the arrest to the press that evening. "This has got to be one of the most exciting days in my entire career,"[62] he said.

A mug shot of Gary Ridgway taken in May 1982.

No Way Out

Although he went quietly, Ridgway denied committing any murders. When read his rights, he asked for an attorney. A defense team was quickly assembled, and through them he let it be known that his DNA had been found on the victims because they were prostitutes. It was just coincidence that they had been killed shortly after he had had sex with them.

In 2002, however, Palenik identified the paint found on the clothing of victims Coffield, Estes, and Bonner and matched it to specks of paint found on a pair of Ridgway's coveralls. The latter had been taken from his locker at Kenworth Truck Company where he worked. The news meant that Ridgway was now linked to seven of the dead girls.

Faced with those facts, even Ridgway's lawyers became convinced their client was hiding the truth. One of them, Mark Prothero, told Ridgway that he would probably be found guilty and sentenced to death if his case went to trial. The attorney remembers: "I outlined the strength of the state's case, along with the difficulty of getting an impartial jury in King County. I did most of the talking. He mostly listened."[63]

Two days later, Ridgway confessed to Prothero that he was the Green River Killer. Armed with that information, Prothero went to King County prosecuting attorney Maleng's office and

Sheriff Dave Reichert, left, personally interrogated Gary Ridgway after his arrest.

AUG/20/2003 WED
9:56:27 AM   A0019

offered to strike a deal. Ridgway would plead guilty to all the murders and give them the whole truth about the cases. In exchange, they would not ask for the death penalty.

The Bargain

Initially, Maleng refused to consider a plea bargain. In his mind, the death penalty was designed for killers such as Ridgway. After consideration, however, he realized that getting Ridgway's confession to all the killings, in addition to learning where many of the victims were still buried, would be extremely beneficial for the families involved.

Maleng also took money into account when opting for a plea bargain. Preparing the case would be extremely expensive, involving millions of dollars. Expert witnesses would have to be hired to testify. Out-of-town witnesses would have to be flown in and put up in motels. Lab analysts would have to work overtime processing evidence, or evidence would have to be sent to outside labs, all at great expense. "It will be a challenge

Prosecutor Norman Maleng accepted a plea bargain from Ridgway in exchange for information about still-missing victims.

for us to find the resources to support this,"[64] said King County budget director Steve Call in December 2001. To add to the cost, Ridgway's lawyers would have to be paid out of public funds, because Ridgway had no private fortune. That meant that King County taxpayers would help foot the bill for his defense, a fact they were sure to resent.

In 2003 Maleng agreed that Ridgway would plead guilty to forty-eight murders and be sentenced to life in prison without the possibility of parole. In return, the killer would help locate remains of his victims and provide other details about the killings. If at any time investigators found that he was lying or holding back information, the deal was off. Reichert expresses his feelings about Maleng's decision:

> I support the prosecutor's courageous decision and am honored to have worked with him to bring this case to conclusion. We can finally let our community know that the Green River Killer can no longer take the lives of our children, a full measure of justice will be imposed on an evil man, and many suffering families can finally know what happened to their daughters.[65]

Ridgway Speaks

With the bargain struck, Ridgway began giving task force members information that opened a window into the life and mind of one of the nation's most malevolent serial killers. For instance, as a child growing up in the Seattle area, Ridgway remembered wanting to kill his mother. She was strong and controlling, while his father was a quiet, easygoing man who simply left the room when his wife became too disagreeable. Gary fantasized about slitting her throat with a kitchen knife, particularly when she shamed him for wetting the bed, a problem

In 2003 Gary Ridgway pled guilty to forty-eight murders and was sentenced to life in prison without the possibility of parole.

he had until he reached his teens. "That would be the ultimate, to, to scar her for life,"[66] he told investigators.

Despite his anger, Ridgway took his father as a model and hid his feelings. In private, however, he acted out. He set small fires, carried out petty thefts, and tortured small animals. These traits characterize sociopaths, persons who exhibit antisocial behavior and have no feelings of empathy or remorse. When he was fifteen or sixteen, he also stabbed a young neighbor boy with a knife. The victim had to be hospitalized and undergo surgery, but Ridgway was never charged with the crime. "He was in the wrong place at the wrong time, and I was in the right place at the right time, I guess what you'd call it,"[67] he told investigators.

Ridgway did poorly in school because he had less than average intelligence. He was also dyslexic. Classes were hard for him, and his mother threatened to put him in a home for the retarded. In high school he was held back twice, finally graduating when he was twenty. Because he was neither smart nor particularly attractive, girls he wanted to date would never pay attention to him. He retaliated by stalking them.

Marriage and Work

After high school Ridgway joined the navy and shortly thereafter married for the first time. During an assignment in the Philippines, he began patronizing prostitutes, a habit he continued for the next thirty years. When he returned from overseas, he discovered his wife had also been unfaithful. In his mind this made her no different than a prostitute, but when she finally left him, he felt angry and betrayed.

Ridgway moved back to the Seattle area in 1971 and found work with the Kenworth Trucking Company, where he was employed for over thirty years. There he felt like he belonged, although coworkers described him as odd. Sometimes he was quiet and reserved. Sometimes he was overly friendly. Diane LaPointe, who worked with him for eight years, remembers how his behavior made many female coworkers uncomfortable:

Hiding in Plain Sight

True-crime writer Ann Rule followed the Green River Killer case with great interest from the beginning. She gives her assessment of the killer, whom she describes as "a boring little man of seemingly predictable habits," in her book Green River, Running Red.

It was Gary Ridgway's protective coloration that let him stay free for more than twenty years. That and his uncommon ability to mask what lay beneath his bland façade, to hide his rage and frustration from his ex-wives, numerous girlfriends, his family, and even the woman who became his third wife. Judith Ridgway appeared to have truly believed that she and Gary "did everything together." She was confident that neither of them had a need for friends or other diversions.

Gary Ridgway was good at only one thing. He was an efficient killer who was so inept at everything else that it was easy for him to hide in plain sight. In a way, he achieved what he had sought for most of his life. At last, people noticed him and he got his name and picture in the paper and on television.

Ann Rule, *Green River, Running Red*. New York: Free Press, 2004, p. 433.

He'd come up and he'd whisper something like, . . . "you'd better not bend over in front of me like that" and then he would . . . turn red and go away like he was embarrassed, ashamed of himself for saying it. . . . [Or] he would come up behind you and stand there until you knew he was there. You would turn around and he would be right there. I'd jump and scream and he thought that was pretty funny and he'd walk off.[68]

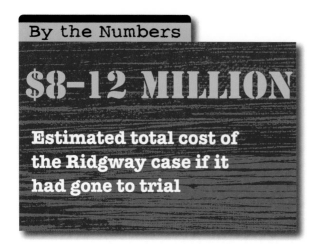

Ridgway married a second time in 1973, but his mother remained a strong force in his life. For instance, she bought all of his clothing for him, and she dictated what he spent his money on. After his son Matthew was born in 1975, Ridgway began going to church regularly, reading his Bible daily, and talking to coworkers about God. This phase of his life ended when his wife, Marcia, filed for divorce in 1980. Ridgway again felt angry and betrayed and later claimed that if he had killed Marcia as he wanted to, he might not have murdered so many other women in the period following the breakup.

In 1988 Ridgway married for a third time. This marriage was the happiest of the three. He and his wife Judith were frugal people who enjoyed going to flea markets. Judith told investigators that he was a loving husband who never even raised his voice to her. Without his wife's knowledge, however, Gary continued to patronize and kill prostitutes, his last murder occurring in 1998. He kept track of the women he "dated" by using a notebook where he coded their names, telephone numbers, and other key information in among grocery lists, work information, and receipts. For instance, a prostitute's name would be paired with a man's name, so she seemed to be part of a couple. If she was African American, he would code her as a "black car."

Confession

Although Ridgway blamed his killing spree on his second wife, he also stated that he deeply resented prostitutes, feeling that they had control over him. "I hated 'em—hated 'em,"[69] he stated. He was not extremely intelligent, but he quickly learned tricks so that no one would suspect he was a killer. For instance, he kept a child's car seat or some toys in his truck, so he appeared to be a nonthreatening family man. At one time he even had his young son with him when he picked up a prostitute. The child's presence did not protect the woman from being murdered a short distance from the vehicle.

Ridgway also made it a point not to kill every prostitute he hired, so that word would get around that he was a safe customer. If he met one of his victims through her boyfriend, he would call the boyfriend a few days after the killing and ask to see the girl again. This gave the impression that he was unaware that she was missing.

No matter who his victim was, he knew how to lull her fears until he moved in for the kill. He preferred strangling, claiming it was more personal and more rewarding. Usually, he reached around her neck from behind and choked her with his arm, but sometimes he used an article of clothing or fishing line. It was easy because he was stronger than they were, and he had the element of surprise on his side. He stated, "The women, they underestimate[d] me. I look like an ordinary person . . . I acted in a way with the . . . prostitutes to make 'em feel more comfortable . . . [I looked like] just an ordinary john, and that was their downfall. . . my appearance was different from what I really was."[70]

The killing was more important to him than the sex because it released some of his rage. He would kill in his truck, in his house, or outdoors. After the kill he would wrap the body in plastic or carpet and take it to a dump site. Then, he took steps to confuse the police and throw them off his trail. For instance, he planted cigarettes by some of

A map showing residences associated with Gary Ridgway.

Digging for evidence

Yesterday, authorities continued searching four South King County residences associated with Gary Leon Ridgway, including calling in a backhoe to excavate the yard at the home where he lived in the early 1980s. The dig turned up no new evidence, officials said.

THE SEATTLE TIMES

85

the bodies. He once left a hair pick, used by African Americans in the 1980s, so the task force would think the killer was black. He dropped the driver's license of one victim at the airport to raise the possibility that she had left town. He even moved bodies. For instance, he killed Denise Bush in Tukwila, Washington, and then transferred parts of her body all the way to Oregon to confuse investigators and involve police from another state.

Even as he tried to confuse investigators, Ridgway hoped that his victims would never be found. This was because he saw them as his private possessions. Long after the kill, he would drive past the dump sites and experience a thrill. When a body was found, it was like a prized object had been snatched away from him. "It felt like they were takin' som'n, some'n a' mine that I put there,"[71] he said.

New Insights into Serial Killers

Ridgway's confessions disgusted investigators. Yet they felt that the process had given them new knowledge about serial killers. Ridgway matched FBI agent Douglas's profile in many ways. Douglas had predicted the murderer would be Caucasian and would have violent fantasies, low self-esteem, and strong religious feelings. He had predicted that there had been discord in the man's home when he was growing up, and that he had had trouble in school. Like Douglas guessed, Ridgway's work involved physical rather than intellectual strength, he was conservative in appearance, and he had a strong interest in police work. In fact, when it came to the latter, Ridgway had wanted to be a policeman but failed the entrance exam. At home he had always been the neighborhood watchdog, keeping an eye out for suspicious activities and reporting them to his neighbors.

Ridgway was not true to the profile in some important respects, however. Contrary to Douglas's predictions, his intelligence was below average, and he led a fairly normal life. He did not take drugs or abuse alcohol, he had a steady job, and he had never before been arrested for violent behavior.

Douglas's mistakes highlighted the fact that investigators could never rely solely on profiling to help them catch a perpetrator. FBI-trained profiler Joel Kohout emphasizes, "I think it's important to point out that profiling is not an exact science. It's merely an investigative tool. Sometimes it's very useful, sometimes not so useful."[72]

Like these young officers, Gary Ridgway dreamed of joining the police force. He failed the entrance exam, however.

Body Hunting

After Ridgway confessed and provided his life history, he had to prove that he was indeed the killer by producing information that only the killer would have. The most telling proof involved leading investigators to spots where he deposited his victims, so they could verify his story and recover bodies that had not yet been found.

The process was done in utmost secrecy, since the task force investigators did not want the media to accompany them on their outings with the killer. Ridgway's hazy memory for the many women he killed complicated the search. Nevertheless,

The Criminal Justice Process

The criminal justice process can be complex and confusing, with many twists and turns along the way. In general, however, a suspect goes through the following steps when he is processed through the criminal justice system.

1 **Arrest:** After an arrest, the defendant is taken to jail and booked (photographed, fingerprinted, and given a receipt for items or money in his possession at the time). After booking is complete, the defendant is placed in a holding cell to await his initial appearance in court.

2 **Appointment** with an attorney: If the defendant cannot afford to hire an attorney and is charged with a crime punishable by imprisonment, an attorney is appointed to represent him.

3 **Arraignment:** Within seventy-two hours of arrest, the defendant is brought before the judge and makes a plea of guilty, not guilty, or no contest. The judge may or may not set bail. If the defendant pleads "not guilty," a date for trial is set.

4 **Trial:** Commonly, the defendant is brought to trial within sixty days if detained in jail or ninety days if out on bail, although preparation time may cause the trial date to be postponed. During trial, the defendant has the right to be present and face his accusers.

5 **Sentencing:** If found guilty, the defendant is again brought before the judge who decides his sentence, taking into account the offense and the defendant's and victims' statements.

6 **Appeal:** If found guilty, a defendant can file an appeal within thirty days of sentencing. An appeal can be based on inadmissible evidence being allowed during the trial, lack of sufficient evidence to support a guilty verdict, or mistakes made by the judge. A court of appeals will then review the case and issue its decision.

he was able to lead investigators to fifty-one different sites, many of which were well known to them. Reichert said of one, "He took me to a site that I [had] spent a lot of time at, and when he stopped at the exact location, it sent chills up my spine."[73]

At some of the unfamiliar sites, new discoveries were made. The bones of Pammy Avent were found on August 16, 2003. On September 2 April Buttram's remains were located. On September 28 Malvar was discovered. The number of sites that Ridgway identified led investigators to believe that he might

Gary Ridgway, wearing cap, and other law enforcement officials search an area of King County, Washington, looking for more sets of remains of victims' bodies.

have committed up to seventy murders. "I find it incredible that an individual was able to cause that many deaths, perpetrate that much suffering and misery on so many people,"[74] said Joe Yellow Robe, father of Patricia Yellow Robe, Ridgway's last victim.

"A Terrible Way to Live"

On December 18, 2003, Joe Yellow Robe and other victims' family members were on hand in a King County courtroom to see Ridgway sentenced to forty-eight life sentences with no possibility of parole. The majority had accepted Maleng's decision to plea bargain in exchange for information. Some however, were angry that Ridgway had escaped death. "I can only hope that someday, someone gets the opportunity to choke you unconscious forty-eight times, so you can live through the horror that you put our daughters, our sisters, our mothers through," shouted Tim Meehan, brother of Mary Meehan. "May God have no mercy on your soul."[75]

Although Gary Ridgway appeared meek and compliant in court, he confessed to more confirmed murders than any other American serial killer.

When the sentencing was over, the convicted man was taken to Washington State Pentitentiary at Walla Walla, Washington, and confined in the Intensive Management Unit (IMU), home to the most dangerous and difficult prisoners. He was locked in a small concrete cell, furnished with a concrete platform, a thin mattress, a stainless steel sink, and a toilet. There he remains, alone, reading his Bible and watching a small black-and-white television which he purchased as a reward for good behavior. He is allowed one hour of exercise a day in the "yard," a 2,100-square foot (195sq m) concrete box with daylight coming in from the top. He has no direct contact with anyone. Despite that, he is never real-

Tim Meehan, brother of Green River Killer victim Mary Meehan, speaks at the sentencing of Gary Ridgway in December 2003.

ly alone. The IMU is always noisy because many inmates are violent, disruptive, and/or mentally ill. The air is filled with yells, screams, and poundings day and night. "It's a terrible way to live,"[76] said Arthur Longworth, a fellow inmate.

While the Green River Killer's life has come to a dead end in prison, others involved in the case go on with theirs. Judith Ridgway lives in seclusion and is planning to write a book. Sarah Christensen, who was five when her mother Carol was killed, works as an orthodontist's assistant and believes she owes it to her mother to be the best person she can be. Reichert was elected to the U.S. Congress in 2004. Jensen is still with the King County Sheriff's Department, working to find names for the remaining unidentified victims.

I'm sorry for killing all those young Ladys. I have tried hard to remember as much as I could to help The detectives find and recover the Ladys. I'm sorry for the scare I put in the community.

I want to Thank the police, prosecutors, my attorneys and all others, that had the patience to work with me and help me remember all the terrible Things I did and to be able to talk about them. I know how horrible my acts were. I have tried for a long time to get these things out of my mind. I have tried for a long time to keep from killing any more ladys. I'm sorry that I've put my wife, my son, my brothers and my family through this hell. I hope that they can find a way to forgive me. I am very sorry for the Ladys that were not found. May they rest in peace. They need a better place than what I gave them. I'm sorry for killing these young Ladys. They had their whole life ahead of them. I am sorry I caused so much pain to so many families.

Gary L Ridgway

Residents of King County will never forget the years the Green River Killer prowled the Strip, looking for victims. Some people continue to believe he should have been put to death. Others simply want to understand him better. They want to figure out how an apparently ordinary little boy, growing up in middle-class America, developed into a deeply disturbed man with no respect or concern for human life. As Reichert stated after Ridgway's sentencing, "He's a monster, he's a killing machine. Period. The scary part is that he's not an alien. He didn't come from Mars. He came from right here in this community."[77]

Notes

Introduction: A Twenty-Year Quest

1. David Reichert, *Chasing the Devil*. New York: Little, Brown, 2004, p. 19.

2. Reichert, *Chasing the Devil*, p. 125.

3. Quoted in Gary Tuchman, "Green River Killer Avoids Death Plea in Deal," CNN.com, November 6, 2003. www.cnn.com/2003/LAW/11/05/green.river.killings.

4. Norman Maleng, "Statement of Norm Maleng on Ridgway Plea," King County Prosecuting Attorney's Office, November 5, 2003. www.metrokc.gov/proatty/news/2003/RidgwPR5.htm.

Chapter One: The Victims: Daughters of the Night

5. Carlton Smith and Tomas Guillen, *The Search for the Green River Killer*. New York: Signet, 2004, p. 86.

6. Smith and Guillen, *The Search for the Green River Killer*, p. 77.

7. Reichert, *Chasing the Devil*, pp. 32–33.

8. Quoted in Ann Rule, *Green River, Running Red*. New York: Free Press, 2004, p. 136.

9. Quoted in Rule, *Green River, Running Red*, p. 89.

10. Reichert, *Chasing the Devil*, pp. 34–35.

11. Quoted in Rule, *Green River, Running Red*, p. 122.

12. Quoted in Joshunda Sanders, "'Survivor' Recounts the Night She Got Away," Seattlepi.com, December 7, 2001. http://seattlepi.nwsource.com/local/49738_guay07.shtml.

13. Reichert, *Chasing the Devil*, p. 297.

14. Reichert, *Chasing the Devil*, p. 190.

Chapter Two: The Investigation: Tracking an Elusive Killer

15. Reichert, *Chasing the Devil*, p. 148.

16. Quoted in Nancy Bartley, "Bruce Kalin Is Back on the Case, and This Time, He's in Charge—the Green River Puzzle Master," *Seattle Times*, February 21, 2002, p. B1.

17. Quoted in Smith and Guillen, *The Search for the Green River Killer*, p. 222.

18. Quoted in Rule, *Green River, Running Red*, p. 179.

19. Quoted in Terry McCarthy, "River of Death," *Time*, June 3, 2002, p. 56.

20. Reichert, *Chasing the Devil*, pp. 49–50.

21. Quoted in www.Mayhem.net, "Green

River Gary," 2006. www.mayhem.net/Crime/greenriver.html.

22. Jon Zonderman, *Beyond the Crime Lab: The New Science of Investigation.* New York: John Wiley & Sons, 1999, p. 130.

23. Quoted in KariSable.com, "Green River Psychological Profile," 2006. www.karisable.com/grprofile.htm.

24. Quoted in Rule, *Green River, Running Red*, p. 272.

25. Reichert, *Chasing the Devil*, p. 153.

26. Reichert, *Chasing the Devil*, p. 129.

27. Reichert, *Chasing the Devil*, p. 141.

28. Quoted in Staff of the *King County Journal, Gary Ridgway: The Green River Killer*. Seattle: King County Publications, 2003, p. 111.

Chapter Three: The Suspects: So Many Possibilities

29. Staff of the *King County Journal, Gary Ridgway*, p. 64.

30. Rule, *Green River, Running Red*, pp. 194–95.

31. Reichert, *Chasing the Devil*, p. 57.

32. Quoted in KariSable.com, "Green River Killer the Falsely Accused," 2006. http://www.karisable.com/grfalse.htm.

33. Reichert, *Chasing the Devil*, p. 62.

34. Quoted in Smith and Guillen, *The Search for the Green River Killer*, p. 142.

35. Reichert, *Chasing the Devil*, pp. 93–94.

36. Quoted in Duff Wilson, Michael A. Barber, and Steve Miletich, "Man Questioned About Green River Murders; House Searched: No Arrest Made." *Seattle Post-Intelligencer,* February 7, 1986, p. A1.

37. Quoted in Rule, *Green River, Running Red*, p. 346.

38. Quoted in www.Mayhem.net, "Green River Gary." www.mayhem.net/Crime/greenriver.html.

39. Quoted in Smith and Guillen, *The Search for the Green River Killer*, p. 463.

40. Quoted in Richard Sevens, "Stevens, Cleared, Still Isn't Talking," *Seattle Times*, December 1, 1989, p. C7.

41. Reichert, *Chasing the Devil*, p. 125.

Chapter Four: The Obstacles: The Case Bogs Down

42. Quoted in Rule, *Green River, Running Red*, p. 175.

43. Quoted in Smith and Guillen, *The Search for the Green River Killer*, p. 229.

44. Smith and Guillen, *The Search for the Green River Killer*, p. 229.

45. Reichert, *Chasing the Devil*, p. 152.

46. Quoted in Rule, *Green River, Running Red*, p. 181.

47. Quoted in Smith and Guillen, *The Search for the Green River Killer*, p. 181.

48. Quoted in Daniel Duggan, "Murders Under a Microscope," Microtrace,

November 11, 2003. www.microtrace
scientific.com/news/copyofarticles/
11_11_03_couriernews/11_11_03_couri
er news.htm.

49. Quoted in Smith and Guillen, *The Search for the Green River Killer*, p. 278.

50. Reichert, *Chasing the Devil*, p. 51.

51. Reichert, *Chasing the Devil*, p. 193.

52. Quoted in Smith and Guillen, *The Search for the Green River Killer*, p. 247.

53. Quoted in Smith and Guillen, *The Search for the Green River Killer*, p. 249.

54. Quoted in Smith and Guillen, *The Search for the Green River Killer*, p. 383.

55. Rule, *Green River, Running Red*, p. 325.

56. Staff of the *King County Journal, Gary Ridgway*, p. 117.

57. Smith and Guillen, *The Search for the Green River Killer*, p. 483.

Chapter Five: Arrest and Confession: The Mind of a Killer

58. Reichert, *Chasing the Devil*, p. 235.

59. Quoted in KariSable.com, "Green River Killer Investigation," 2006. www.karis able.com/grinv.htm.

60. Reichert, *Chasing the Devil*, p. 237.

61. Reichert, *Chasing the Devil*, p. 243.

62. Quoted in Jamie Swift, "Auburn Man Arrested in Green River Killings: Gary L. Ridgway Arrested in Renton Nearly Two

Decades After Serial Murders," *South County Journal*, December 1, 2001, p. 1.

63. Quoted in Carlton Smith, "The Devil We Now Know," *Seattle Weekly*, November 12, 2003. www.seattleweek ly.com/news/0346/031112_news_green river.php.

64. Quoted in Alex Fryer and Carol M. Ostrom, "Cost of Trying Ridgway Likely in the Millions—DNA Tests, Hiring Officers and Lawyers Part of Expenses," *Seattle Times*, December 8, 2001, p. B1.

65. Quoted in King County Sheriff's Office, "Prosecutor and Sheriff Announce Plea Agreement," 2006. www.metrokc.gov /sheriff/news/green_river/press.

66. Quoted in Reichert, *Chasing the Devil*, p. 274.

67. Quoted in Staff of the *King County Journal, Gary Ridgway*, p. 19.

68. Quoted in KariSable.com, "Gary Leon Ridgway: Employee," 2006. www.karis able.com/greenrivergrwork.htm.

69. Quoted in Rule, *Green River, Running Red*, p. 391.

70. Quoted in Smith and Guillen, *The Search for the Green River Killer*, p. 520.

71. Quoted in Staff of the *King County Journal, Gary Ridgway*, p. 43.

72. Quoted in David Weber, "Experts Play Down Expectations in Serial Killer Probe," *PM*, November 9, 2004. www. abc.net.au/pm/content/2004/s1239582. htm.

73. Quoted in KIROTV.com, "Task Force Members Recount Chilling Search," November 7, 2003. www.kirotv.com/greenrivermurders/2618569/detail.html.

74. Quoted in Tuchman, "Green River Killer Avoids Death Plea in Deal."

75. Quoted in Smith and Guillen, *The Search for the Green River Killer*, p. 524.

76. Quoted in Karen O'Leary, "A Look at Ridgway's Life Behind Bars," KIRO7 News, March 3, 2004. www.officer.com/news/IBS/kiro/news-2035289.html.

77. Quoted in Liza Javier and Ellen Lang, "Ridgway Faces Victims' Families," King5.com, December 18, 2003. www.king5.com/sharedcontent/northwest/greenriver/stories/NW_121803WABridgwaysentenceLJ.b45e0a45.html.

For More Information

Books

David Reichert, *Chasing the Devil*. New York: Little, Brown, 2004. The story of the Green River Killer, told by one of the men who tracked and apprehended him.

Ann Rule, *Green River, Running Red*. New York: Free Press, 2004. Renowned crime writer Ann Rule gives insights into the lives of the victims in this work on the Green River Killer.

Staff of the *King County Journal*, *Gary Ridgway: The Green River Killer*. Seattle: King County Publications, 2003. The story of America's most prolific serial killer is recounted by reporters who covered the case from beginning to end.

Periodicals

Tomas Guillen and Carlton Smith, "Amid the Confusion, a Task Force Is Born," *Seattle Times*, September 17, 1987, p. A1.

———, "A Case That Kept Eluding the Police: Police Slow to Act on Their Suspicions," *Seattle Times*, September 15, 1987, p. A1.

———, "Couple Finds a 'Black Hole' in Search for Missing Daughter," *Seattle Times*, September 15, 1987, p. A9.

———, "Green River: What Went Wrong? Police at First Failed to Notice Pattern," *Seattle Times*, September 13, 1987, p. A1.

———, "Police Net Catches the Wrong Man," *Seattle Times*, September 16, 1987, p. A1.

———, "A Setting Made for Murderer: Prostitution Provided the Setting for a Killer," *Seattle Times*, September 14, 1987, p. A1.

———, "What Kind of a Man Would Murder 46 Women?" *Seattle Times*, September 18, 1987, p. A10.

Terry McCarthy, "River of Death," *Time*, June 3, 2002, p. 56.

Jamie Swift, "Auburn Man Arrested in Green River Killings: Gary L. Ridgway Arrested in Renton Nearly Two Decades After Serial Murders," *South County Journal*, December 1, 2001, p. 1.

Internet Sources

Carlton Smith, "The Devil We Now Know," *Seattle Weekly*, November 12, 2003. www.seattleweekly.com/news/0346/0311 12_news_greenriver.php.

Web Sites

Court TV's Crime Library (www.crimeli brary.com/index.html). Gives in-depth coverage of serial killers and other notorious criminals.

Green River Killer Website (www.green riverkiller.com). Gives information about the Green River Killer and other suspects.

Kari Sable's True Crime and Justice Website (www.karisable.com/crime.htm). Includes true crime book reviews and information and discussion on serial killers and other topics.

Index

Picture Credits

Cover image (main): Josh Trujillo-Pool/Getty Images

© Anthony Bolante/Reuters/Corbis, 72

AP Images, 8, 28, 31, 39, 43, 60, 63, 66, 76, 78, 79, 89, 90, 91, 92

Courtesy Seattle Post-Intelligencer, 23

© David Gard/Star Ledger/Corbis, 87

© Elaine Thompson/Pool/Reuters/Corbis, 17

© Gregor Schuster/Zefa/Corbis, 65

© Henry Diltz/Corbis, 44

© Jerry McCrea/Star Ledger/Corbis, 75

© Jim Craigmyle/Corbis, 54

© Matthew McVay/Corbis, 33, 36, 57

Photograph by Bryan Monroe. The Seattle Times, 1987. Reproduced by permission, 7

Photograph by Dale Blindheim. The Seattle Times, 1984. Reproduced by permission, 13

Photograph by Matt McVay. The Seattle Times, 1984. Reproduced by permission, 19

Photograph by Michele Lee McMullen. The Seattle Times. Reproduced by permission, 18

Photograph by Richard S. Heyza. The Seattle Times, 1986. Reproduced by permission, 42

Photograph. The Seattle Times. Reproduced by permission, 85

© POOL/Elaine Thompson/Reuters/Corbis, 81

© Reuters/Corbis, 77

© Robert Essel NYC/Corbis, 15, 50

©Roger Ressmeyer/Corbis, 37

©Royalty Free/Corbis, 53

About the Author

Diane Yancey lives in the Pacific Northwest with her husband, Michael; their dog, Gelato; and their cats, Lily and Newton. She has written more than twenty-five books for middle-grade and high school readers, including *Murder* and *The Forensic Anthropologist*.